THE COMPLETE
GUIDE TO
PALMISTRY

THE COMPLETE GUIDE TO PALMISTRY

THE MYSTERY OF YOUR PALM

How it Affects Your Life, Your Career, Your Marriage

By PSYCHOS

LONDON
W. FOULSHAM & CO. LTD.
NEW YORK · TORONTO · CAPE TOWN · SYDNEY

W. FOULSHAM & CO. LTD.,
Yeovil Road, Slough, Berks., England.

ISBN 0-572-00038-3

PRINTED IN GREAT BRITAIN AT
THE CAMELOT PRESS LTD, SOUTHAMPTON

CONTENTS

PAGE

INTRODUCTION   7

PART ONE

CHEIROGNOMY: CHARACTER AS SHOWN BY THE HANDS IN GENERAL

CHAPTER I

CONSISTENCY AND FLEXIBILITY   9

CHAPTER II

THE PALM AND ITS INDICATIONS   12

CHAPTER III

THE FINGER AND FINGER TIPS   16

CHAPTER IV

THE THUMB AND NAILS   35

CHAPTER V

THE MOUNTS   45

CONTENTS

PART TWO

CHEIROMANCY: PAST, PRESENT AND FUTURE EVENTS AS INDICATED BY THE LINES AND MARKS ON THE HANDS

CHAPTER VI   PAGE

THE CHARACTERISTICS OF LINES 72

CHAPTER VII

THE LINES 82

CHAPTER VIII

THE MINOR LINES 133

CHAPTER IX

THE PROFESSIONS 145

CHAPTER X

GENERAL INSTRUCTIONS 154

THE COMPLETE GUIDE TO PALMISTRY

INTRODUCTION

THE human hand has been described as the Creator's masterpiece of mechanism, in its wonderful adaptation to the requirements of life ; yet, strange to say, whilst almost every section of the human body has its medical specialists, there are none such for the hands as a whole.

Medical men occasionally use the nails and fingers to confirm a diagnosis ; but few of them realise that the hand —as the direct servant of the brain—in its markings, not only reveals the workings of the brain and the general characteristics, but also the physical ailments ; further, any latent heart weakness is plainly and certainly discernable in the hand.

It cannot be denied that there is much opposition to the practice of Palmistry, based upon ignorance and bigotry. On the other hand, I dare venture to affirm that He who veined the leaves of trees and plants so that the skilled botanist could read their story from the lines in the leaves, has so lined the human palm that the scientist can with equal facility read therein the story of the human life.

No two hands are alike, and they are so marked that they constitute a veritable chart of the life ; all that a man needs to know of himself, his capabilities, his faults and feelings, and the probable outcome of his life, is therein set forth in a manner at once plain, simple and easy to understand. To the trained reader, the hand reveals the character, talents and proclivities, as well as indicating the most suitable career to be followed, the health, sickness, and important incidents of life, as they affect the position and welfare.

It has, I am aware, been recklessly asserted by some so-called scientists that the lines are merely creases formed by the folding of the hands ; but this contention is easily refuted, by an inspection of the hands—your own, for instance—which will disclose lines in positions utterly at variance with so puerile a contention.

Notwithstanding the marvellous construction of the hand, it cannot, of itself, perform one single act—all that it does is by order of the brain, the seat of every mental operation, and it is entirely dependent on the brain for its intelligence, and therefore, being its servant, it reflects the kind of brain behind it.

It must be understood that Cheirosophy, or Palmistry, is in no way connected with occultism—it is usually divided into two sections, viz. : Cheirognomy, or the science of reading character from the shape of the hand and fingers; and Cheiromancy, the science of reading the actions and habits, the past, present and future events from the formation of the palm and the lines marked thereon. This division of the science, however, is by no means arbitrary ; on the contrary they are but parts of one whole, and it is only adopted for the convenience of students. In Cheirognomy, the hands are recognised as belonging to, or coming under one or more of seven classes or types, a matter which will be fully explained later. At the outset, however, I shall follow the course generally adopted, and deal with the general features of the hand which carry with them their own significance to whatever type or combination of types the hand may belong.

PART ONE

CHEIROGNOMY or CHARACTER as shown by the HANDS IN GENERAL

CHAPTER I

CONSISTENCY AND FLEXIBILITY

In all examinations, it is necessary to note both hands, otherwise there will be failure, due to the fact that men change as they grow older, and such changes will be marked in the right hand, unless the person under examination is left-handed, when the change will be marked in the left or operative hand. It is a matter of general experience that the left hand describes the natural man, while the right hand records the changes, in a right-handed subject. This one item alone suffices to indicate whether the course of the life has been stationary, progressive, or retrograde.

In this examination the first point to be noted is the TEXTURE of the skin ; this will be best ascertained by feeling the back of the hand, and noting its softness or otherwise. Texture will give a knowledge of your client's refinement. If it is fine, soft and delicate, it will tell of a refined, sensitive nature which will mark everything he does—the coarse and common will repel. The coarser the skin the coarser the nature and qualities ; this shows a lack of refinement or sensibility, and often adds a tyrannical disposition. A medium development—neither fine nor coarse—is often met and constitutes a balance between the two extremes.

The next point to be noted is the CONSISTENCY of the hands, i.e., their softness or hardness under press re. This will tell the amount of energy possessed The thing to ascertain is the hardness, softness, flabbiness or resilience of the hand. This consistency comes under one of four heads : there is the Hard hand, which belongs to the lesser intelligence, and with these the texture will usually be coarse. This hand does not yield to pressure, has no elasticity or spring—the subject will be active, work is no burden to him—the brain will be dense and the subject will be unprogressive.

There is the hand which, as you press it, feels as though it were made of rubber—it is essentially the active hand and is possessed by those who do not merely talk but who act. It indicates one who has life, energy, push and vigour, and it is marked by intelligence.

The hand which, when grasped, feels as though it would squeeze through your fingers, is the flabby hand ; this tells of a deficiency in physical energy—a dreamer, idle, luxurious, lazy.

There is an intermediate consistency known as soft ; the hand will not have the boneless feeling of the flabby hand, yet it will be soft, and its owner, though deficient in energy, is not exactly lazy and energy may be aroused. Both hands must be noted, as if the left is soft and the right elastic, you can tell of the development of energy ; but if the left is elastic or hard, and the right soft, then laziness has set in and success will be remote.

Very little practice will suffice to enable the reader to distinguish between the respective consistencies, and this can be done even in shaking hands ; if the acquaintance is known to the reader, the respective qualities may easily be verified by this simple test.

When testing the hands to ascertain the consistency, you will notice that, in some cases, the hand will be stiff and hard to open, the fingers curving in towards the palm. This will indicate one who is cautious in all that he does, and entirely wanting in adaptability—stiff, hard and unyielding in all his ways, this hand is usually hard in its consistency.

Others you will find that open easily, and the fingers naturally straighten themselves to the full extent, and may under pressure bend slightly backward. This is a normal development of the hand, and the owner of it is one who does not go to extremes, but is broad, earnest, sympathetic and well-balanced.

Again you will meet one in which the fingers easily and

painlessly bend back till they almost form an arch. This is the pliable, or flexible hand, and it tells of a mind susceptible to keen impressions, versatile and adaptable, sympathetic, liberal in generosity to a fault. This full flexibility makes for mental brilliancy. Where, however, the fingers only bend back at the first, or nail, phalanges, and the rest of the fingers remain normal, only mental flexibility will be indicated. Both hands should be noted as to flexibility, in order to estimate the character of the progress made, if any.

CHAPTER II

A GREAT difference will be seen in the palm of the hands, and the various characters of the palms indicate the various characteristics of their owners.

If the palm is thin, skinny and narrow, it tells of one timid, weak-minded, with narrowness of views and paucity of intellect, as well as a want of depth of character, energy, mental and moral force. If accompanied with long thin fingers, it will indicate a tyrannical disposition.

If the palm is in proportion with the fingers and thumb and the general physique, firm without hardness, of elastic consistency without flabbiness, it will indicate an evenly balanced mind, ready to receive impressions, appreciative, intelligent and able to sustain and carry out the promptings of instinct. But if over developed in its proportions, it will tend to produce over-confidence, selfishness and sensuality, especially if the development is towards the base of the hand. If this hand is hard, with the palm longer than the fingers, the character will have a trend towards brutality and animal propensities, unless restrained by other indications, such as a strong thumb and a good head line.

The palm should be normal and in proportion to the thumb and fingers and the general physique, otherwise it indicates a modification of the signs on the rest of the hand.

If the palm is flabby and soft, it will indicate indolence, mental or physical, and a love of ease, luxury and pleasure; opportunities will be missed from sheer laziness.

If thick and firm, while the colour is approaching white, there will be selfishness and coldness of disposition. If high and hard, it exaggerates the Plain of Mars, and indicates aggressiveness and a quarrelsome disposition.

A hollow palm denotes misfortune, losses, misery, and a prospect of failure in enterprises and undertakings, as it occasions a serious defection of the Plain of Mars. It is undoubtedly an indication of ill-luck, no matter how favourable the rest of the hand may be—there is a want of forcefulness.

This hollowness of the palm will often be found to incline to one or other of the lines, or portion of the hand, more than to another, and according to its position in the hand, the cause will be indicated. If falling under the Life Line, it will be found that domestic trouble is experienced. If under the Line of Saturn, disappointment in business or the career has caused it. If under the Heart Line, sadness and grief through the affections is the cause.

If the hollow is under an Influence Line joining the Line of Saturn, which with other indications point to marriage, then the marriage will have been a disappointment sufficient to mar the life, or a broken engagement will have been experienced.

In all cases, the consistency of the hand, whether flabby, soft, elastic or hard, should be noted, together with the character of the thumb and finger tips and the length and condition of the Head Line.

THE HAND AS A WHOLE

The appearance of the hand as a whole will show whether it is evenly balanced, or is heavier or lighter in some parts than in others.

In this examination the Three Worlds of Palmistry make their appearance. These worlds are based on the presumption that a person is guided by mind, by the affairs of everyday life (the material), or by the baser and animal instincts (the passions).

Taking the hand as a whole, the fingers or the upper portion represent mind, the middle portion of the hand (from the base of the fingers to a line running across the hand from the top of Mount Luna to Mount Venus) represents the material, while the base of the hand (from the line above described to the wrist) shows the lower elements. These constitute the Three Worlds of Palmistry.

Modern palmists, however, prefer to divide the fingers and the palm each into the three Kingdoms of Mind, Material, or Animal—this is fully described in Chapter III.

If in the outstretched hand, the length of the fingers predominates, then Mind will be the ruling force. If the middle section is most developed then the world of business (the Material) is prominent. If the lower section predominates, the subject lives on a low level and is sensual, with strong animal instincts.

Assuming that the world of Mind is predominant, then the subject is fitted for study, for some mental occupation ; if this predominance is very marked, without anything to support it, then the subject will be one who lives in a realm of ideas, without having sufficient of the material or practical side to keep him from following ideals to the exclusion of the necessary practical matters. This explains why so many literary men, tutors and students, are such poor business men, and accumulate nothing.

The middle world is the practical one, combining the qualities of ambition, soberness, wisdom, shrewdness, aggression and resistence. This predominance, if in excess of *both* the upper and lower worlds, shows that business, practical life, and material success, is the sphere in which the subject operates. Thus he would be well fitted for commerce, politics, agriculture, or any practical pursuit, money getting being the aim.

The lower world developed will show the subject to be one who lives in the realm of base desires, and enjoys himself best when gratifying his sensual impulses. This will be particularly true if the hand is also coarse. Such a type can appreciate nothing elevating ; if he acquires money, he cannot make a refined use of it. The vulgar and showy attract him ; he revels in display, and in his home will be profusion, but no taste. He is vulgar and common in his tastes—he lives in the lower world.

These developments are found in all hands. It is possible, however, to see hands in which you cannot at sight tell which world predominates. This is a fortunate sign, as it shows the balanced hand, a person who is not one-sided in his views of life, but is intelligent, wise, practical and prudent. This balance of the Three Worlds makes for success, but consistency must be considered, for laziness can counterbalance ability and good intentions.

In order to secure worldly success, the Middle World must show good development. Mind may win renown and glory—but no money ; or the base qualities may be strong, yet not prevent financial success. Link the two Upper Worlds, then financial success will result from mental strength; link the two lower ones, and money can be made though it may be in coarse occupations. Take away the middle portion and you then have mental power combined with coarse instincts ; lacking commonsense, such a development cannot make for success. Look to the balanced hand for the best results ; next to the hand having either the Upper or Lower in combination with the Middle World.

The best way to carry out this examination is to have both hands laid wide open, with the palms uppermost and the fingers straightened to their *natural* length. This will give you a full view of the hands, and you can then note whether the fingers are seemingly long enough to balance the palm, or whether they are short than the palm, or appear to be much longer. This will show you whether the hand is in perfect balance or not.

CHAPTER III

THE FINGERS AND FINGER TIPS

THE fingers must next come under examination, in order to ascertain whether they are normal in length, long or short, and whether the joints are knotty or smooth— as also the character of the Tips, and whether spatulate, square, conic, or pointed.

The practice of speaking of hands as being spatulate, square, conic, or pointed is entirely erroneous, for the fingers cannot be classed in a group. Each one must be considered by itself, as hands are almost always mixed in type, and you will find that the finger tips will be seen to vary greatly in shape.

Each finger is named from, and takes the quality of the Mount under it. Thus the first, or index finger is named Jupiter, the second finger is Saturn, the third is named Apollo, while the fourth, or little finger, is named Mercury. The thumb is not considered as a finger ; it is so important that it stands in a class by itself.

In examining the fingers, the first point to notice is their length. If any doubt is felt as to their length, let the subject close the fingers over the palm so as to ascertain how far towards the wrist they reach. Generally speaking, they should, if long, reach to the wrist, but allowance must be made for the Mounts at the base of the fingers lessening their reach.

As a general rule, in practice, whenever the fingers extend anywhere below the centre of the Mount of Venus towards the wrist I class them as long and apply long-fingered qualities to them.

When the question of their length has been satisfactorily established, the next point will be to observe the joints at the back of the fingers, in order to see if they are Knotty or Smooth, and also whether the first or second

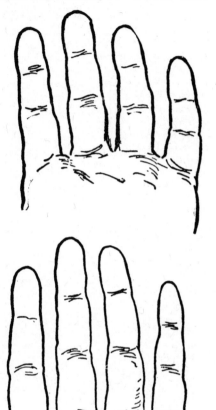

SHORT FINGERS—ABOVE
LONG FINGERS—BELOW

joints, or both of them, are prominent or knotty, and apply knotty or smooth qualities accordingly.

Then note, by pressing backwards, the flexibility of each individual finger ; if one is more flexible than the others, the qualities of the Mount for which it stands will be strong. Fingers bent laterally always increase the shrewdness of the Mount qualities ; whilst a finger which twists on its axis discloses a liability to the moral or physical defects of its Mount—to determine which, an inspection of the particular Mount, the lines marked on it, the nails, the Life Line, and the Line running to the Mount, is essential.

The tips of the fingers must, individually, be noted, and spatulate, square, conic or pointed qualities applied to the finger and its Mount. Notice also whether any finger appears to stand more erect than the others, with one or more of the other fingers leaning towards it—this erect finger will be the strongest, as every finger leaning towards another gives some of its strength to the finger to which it leans. Fingers, to be well-balanced, should be set evenly on the palm, as, if low set, the strength of its Mount is reduced, while a high-set finger increases the strength of its Mount.

You must also note whether the fingers are close together at their base, or if there is a space between them. If the space between the thumb and the side of the hand s very wide, it will indicate one who is generous, a lover of freedom and independence, and who chafes under restraint. The fingers of Jupiter and Saturn separating widely show a carelessness of conventionalism : a person who is not bound down by the views of others but who will form his or her own opinions. The fingers of Saturn and Apollo being widely separated show one careless as to the future, and with a trend to extravagance and not stiff in manner. The fingers of Apollo and Mercury widely separated indicate independence in action, one who will do as he or she wishes, regardless of what others may think.

When you find all the fingers widely separated, you may expect free thought, Bohemianism, and freedom of action, some one easy to get acquainted with, and utterly

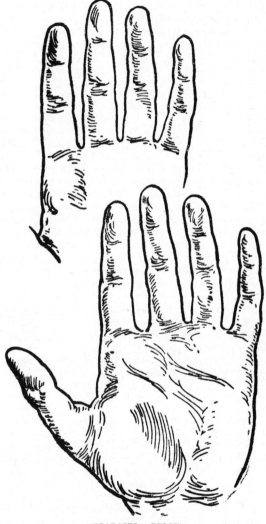

SEPARATED—BELOW
CLOSE—ABOVE

indifferent to the opinions of Mrs. Grundy. If all the fingers lie bunched together, you will have an individual difficult to get acquainted with, very stiff, a slave to formality, stingy and self-centred, smoewhat suspicious.

The respective phalanges, or sections of the fingers, are counted first, second or third from the tips of the fingers downwards towards the palm. Here in these phalanges, in my opinion, are the Three Worlds of Palmistry— the mental, abstract or material, and the animal propensities ; they sustain the qualities of the Mount, and show whether they will be used in the mental, practical, or physical worlds.

The first (nail) phalanx, if longest, shows that the mental will rule. The second, when longest and largest, tells us that the business side will predominate in the subject. If the third is strongest, it indicates the predominance of the material qualities, and that coarseness or brutishness may be expected—the subject is largely absorbed in the physical side of his or her life.

The longer the first phalanx the more closely will mental matters absorb the attention. With the second phalanx long and thick, the money-making side will lead ; while if the third phalanx is very long and thick, a great love of eating and drinking, luxury and pleasure will predominate.

If, however, the third phalanx, instead of being thick is long, narrow and waist-like in shape, then the subject only cares for money for what it will buy. He may have an enquiring turn of mind—this is shown by the chinks between the fingers. If the fingers are very long and the chinks very wide, he will pry into everyone's affairs from sheer curiosity.

In the study of the fingers, the shape of the tips must be considered as to their bearing and effect on the qualities of the respective fingers, in order to dissect thoroughly the character of the subject.

FINGER TIPS

To speak of types of *Hands* is not only misleading, but is distinctly erroneous, as you will seldom find a hand containing all the fingers of the same class of character,

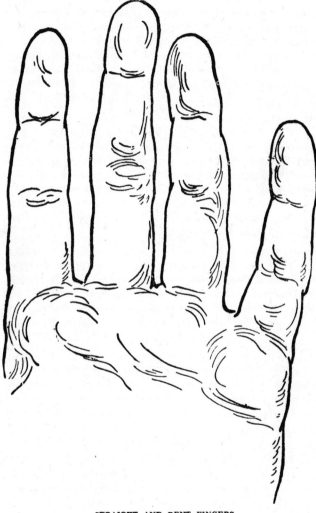

STRAIGHT AND BENT FINGERS

Hence finger tips are classed as spatulate, i.e., broad and flat-looking, square, conic or rounded, or pointed, according as they appear to the eye.

The Spatulate tip is the broadest ; its possessor always seeks the practical and commonsense side of things, and is ever on the go, inspiring others with enthusiasm and activity. He is fond of sports, manual exercises, animals, and makes an excellent emigrant. He is a strong lover and is constant and true.

The Spatulate tip also shows great originality. This man does not follow any well-ordered system or established rules, but likes to find out new ways of doing things, and he invents new machines. Independent, he goes his own way through life, caring little what others may say of him. He will not only discover, but build up and develop new lands. Everywhere he is a power in activity, originality and enterprise.

The Square tip is one which is distinctly square at the ends of the fingers, and indicates order, system, arrangement and regularity in everything. Disorder is to them an abomination, whether in the home, shop or office. They think and act by rule, and love punctuality in all. They are polite, strict observers of social customs, and resent any breach of accustomed forms. It is the useful tip, and marks the good book-keeper, clerk, merchant, librarian, secretary, mathematician and scientist. These tips, as in the case of the Spatulate, add their qualities to each individual finger and Mount. In addition to the foregoing, the Square tips are skilful in all games where precision and accuracy are an essential ; hence they are often good shots, as well as being careful in dress, and methodical in habits.

The Conic tip in shape forms a distinct cone at the end of the fingers, and it has many degrees of development. When the cone is not pronounced, there will be less of the Conic qualities, and it will partake of the Square or Spatulate. The Conic tip reveals a nature artistic, impulsive, intuitive, quick and impressionable, one to whom the beautiful and harmonious strongly appeal. To these tips the precision, regularity and punctuality of the Square tip is a nuisance and a restraint.

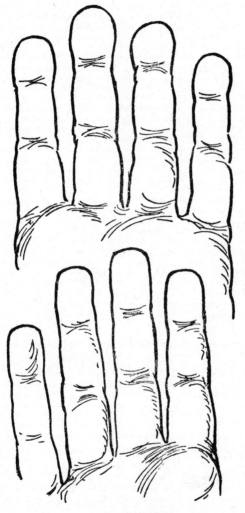

SPATULATE—ABOVE
SQUARE—BELOW

Conic tips possess talent, quickness of mind, and great intuitiveness—this natural intuition, though one of their greatest gifts, is also an element of danger, as they are often led by it against the dictates of reasons. They are emotional and sympathetic, easily influenced, and as a result, they are not constant in their love affairs.

Pointed tips once seen, can never be mistaken for others, as their long, narrow and excessively pointed build cannot be forgotten. There is nothing of a practical nature in these Pointed tips ; all is inspirational and idealistic, and their possessors live in dreamland. To them the beautiful is everything. They may be seen in all classes of society, but wherever found it will indicate one who is a dreamer and unpractical, one to whom life is a continual disappointment, unless they happen to possess the means to indulge their constantly changing fancies.

In dealing with all classes of Tips, it must be borne in mind that a soft hand will make the Spatulate tip only a lover of action, not one to indulge in it personally. It will also decrease the force of Square tips and add considerably to the idealism of Conic and Pointed tips. The energy shown by the elastic consistency of the hand, as well as a strong thumb, will be necessary to bring out the greatest possibilities of the tips.

Turning to the other side of the hand, the backs of the fingers will impress you as belonging to one of two classes— those having the joints of the phalanges developed and Knotty, or those which are Smooth. These two general classes are again divided into those which have *both* joints Knotty, and those where only one joint is thickened.

Two distinctly opposite classes of people are indicated by these Knotty or Smooth fingers. On many fingers the first joints only are developed ; this development is known as the Knot of Mental order, and gives order in ideas and arrangement of thought.

On other hands we find the second Joints of the fingers developed, and these are known as the Knots of Material order, which give punctuality and neatness in the home, office and general surroundings.

The development of both Knots on the fingers show both Mental and Material order and system ; it gives the

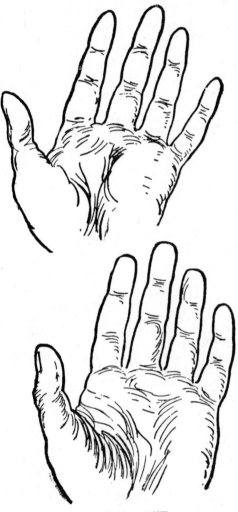

POINTED—ABOVE
CONIC—BELOW

indication of one who acts slowly, thinks carefully over things, and applies the attributes of mental and material order to whatever he does. Naturally this leads to the habit of analyzing everything, and reasoning out all questions, hence they are not carried away by impulse or enthusiasm, but investigate all things ; they are studious, and they always give an impression of quiet energy and commonsense.

If only the Knot of Mental order is developed, it will indicate the possession of an intelligent mind, a systematic way of thinking, mental carefulness and regularity— providing the Knot is of normal size. Excessive development produces cranks, or even insanity.

If the second or Knot of Material order only is seen well developed, it will tell of one whose home is neat and orderly ; the personal appearance will be neat, and the subject will be methodical in his life and habits. If the tips of the fingers are Square, he will be carried away by his sense of system.

When Knotty fingers are seen, the tips of the fingers must always be noted. If these are Square tips, they add Square qualities to the Knotty ones—in this case you will find a fanatic for red-tape, a severe disciplinarian and hard task-master. If the Tips are Spatulate, with the first Knot developed, you will have a subject who is extremely obstinate and cranky. Conic or Pointed tips lessen the force of the Knots, and constitute the ideal Knotty hand.

The consistency of the hand must be noted, as the Knots require the elastic consistency for their fullest expression.

If the Knots bulge so as to distort the fingers, the characteristics will be very pronounced ; while if they bulge out at the sides of the fingers, as well as on the back, it is an excessive development, as it will cause the first phalanx of the finger to bend inwards, in which case the stiff qualities of the mind will predominate and hobbies will be ridden to death.

Many hands will be found which are distinctly Smooth in appearance, no Knots being seen on the fingers. The fingers may have any sort of tips, and to them belong

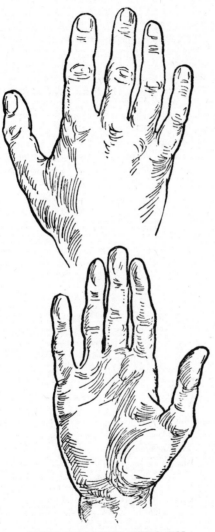

HANDS WITH MIXED FINGER TIPS

impulse, intuition and inspiration.   Sentiment and fancy, rather than reason, will guide their actions, and invariably with them first impressions are the best and the safest to follow.   They are artistic in their taste, quick to think, and act always by inspiration.   They love the things which please the eyes, are tasteful in dress, but if the fingers are coarse and thick, this may degenerate into a love of show and display.   These qualities do not belong solely to high-grade characters ; they are to be found in the lowest walks of life.   Smooth fingers always indicate one who relies, not on reason, but on inspiration, impulse and intuition, who loves the beautiful according to his or her standard, and who in general acts on the spur of the moment.

Smooth-fingered persons are emotional, and far more susceptible to and influenced by passion (not temper) than those with Knotty fingers.   They are successful in business and life, yet there is an element of danger and uncertainty about them, for their inspirations are often wrong.   A good Head Line is needed to ensure safety with the Smooth-fingered individual.

Smooth fingers with the first joint marked by a Knot often denote a talent for invention, or intuition in science.

If the Head Line is defective and twisted, and declines on the Mount of Luna, with a short second phalanx of the Thumb, though intuition remains, it will generally be wrong and lead to false conceptions.

The Tips of the Smooth fingers must be taken into account.   If Pointed, the most artistic side of the Smooth fingers is indicated.   If Square, the quickness and inspiration will be on practical lines.   If Spatulate, it will add originality, independence and activity, but such a combination will need very careful handling to prevent the subject from becoming a crank and consequently unsuccessful in life.

Again the fingers should be noted for their Length, as they will be either long, normal or short.   The category under which they come may be tested in the manner previously described, by closing the fingers over the palm so as to ascertain how far towards the wrist they will reach.

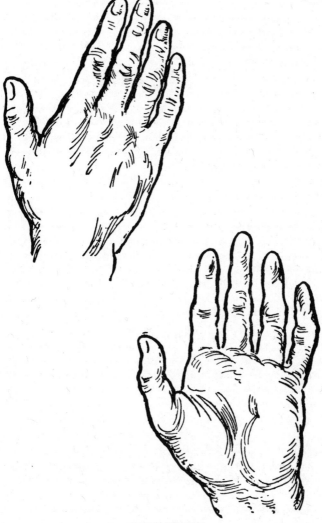

KNOTTY FINGERS

Long hands are to be met with in which the palm as well as the fingers will be very long, though the fingers may be but a trifle over normal length. These Long hands tell of one who is not only slow-going, but also talks slowly and carefully enunciates every syllable of his words. The long hands indicate the possession of a mind that acts slowly and they must be taken in connection with long fingers.

A great difference will be found in the character of those with long thin fingers and those with long thick fingers. Thin fingers accentuate the qualities of long fingers. Thick fingers make long fingers less given to pushing long-fingered qualities to excess.

The long-fingered person is one who goes closely into details, accepts nothing as a whole, is very careful in small things but often allows large ones to pass unnoticed, and is always more or less suspicious and easily offended. He is careful in all things, very sensitive, and neat in appearance. As a rule he possesses a good memory and makes a good book-keeper; in fact in any office where accuracy and attention to detail is essential he is at home. With Square tips, their regularity and detail will make the possessor an ideal accountant.

If the long finger is Smooth, it will not take them so long to grasp ideas ; but if Knotty it will mean an added love of minute detail and analysis—patient plodders always. In music they are successful from carefulness and close observation of the score ; in conversation they are apt to be prolix and tedious, in literature exact. In art, their pictures will show every detail of their subject. In home life they study comfort and are thoughtful, watchful and careful.

They have their failings, amongst them being slowness and tediousness ; often they are bores and frequently selfish. Their fingers and short critical nails will accentuate this, and the owners may be considered selfish, particularly if either the Mounts of Venus or Apollo are undeveloped.

Long fingers are cold-blooded, unsympathetic, and are by no means ready to grant favours nor are they always true to the affections. If long and thin, they are sus-

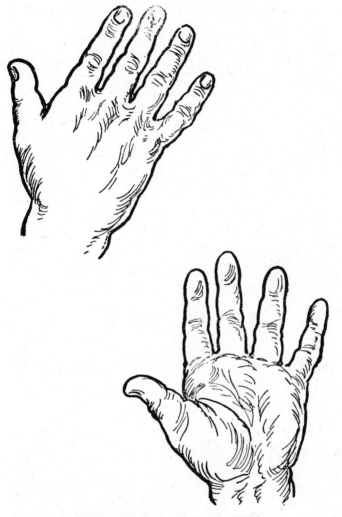

ELEMENTARY OR UNDEVELOPED HANDS

picious and resentful ; those of the thick long fingers will be truer.

The Tips must be considered when studying long fingers. If Spatulate, activity and originality will move them and amongst such will be found inventors and explorers ; the qualities of the Spatulate tips must be added to the sense of detail, and this combination constitutes the best indication of originality. The Square tip is too much under the control of routine and custom to be original. If the tips are Conic, long fingers will turn to art and love of the beautiful, and the Conic qualities must be added to them.

The long fingers will be found in all walks of life, the ignorant and the educated ; in dealing with them, it must be remembered that though they do not stand for the same degree of fineness, they tell of detail. These long fingers do the finer mechanical work, and often belong to delicate engravers.

The next type to be considered will be the Short fingers. These are found among all classes and in both sexes. Short fingers will scarcely reach to the centre of the Mount of Venus, but they may vary in degree of shortness according to the length of the palm. The shorter they are the more pronounced are their qualities.

The qualities of Short fingers are the reverse of Long ones. They think quickly, and if very short, like a flash, and act accordingly. They are highly intuitive, and quickly judge whether you are telling the truth or not. No question of analysis or detail troubles them. Things as a whole are what they deal with. They are impulsive and act on the spur of the moment; they run the risk of making mistakes through jumping to conclusions. Hotheaded, and once started, they push diligently their enterprises.

Short-fingered people are only satisfied when doing big things—they build huge buildings and bridges, plan gigantic enterprises, lead armies, control large concerns, but leave details to long-fingers. They are as a rule quick-witted and very concise in their expressions, and have the faculty of saying much in little.

The Pointed tip, giving ideality, fervour, impressionability and indifference, is an element of danger to them, as it increases their impulsiveness and leads to excess.   Conic tips are not quite so dangerous, but they emphasise the qualities.

Square tips decrease impressionability and lessen impetuosity.   Spatulate tips add activity and originality, and are not so good for Short fingers as Square tips. Flexibility of the hand adds elasticity of mind, and increases the Short-fingered qualities ; giving as it does greater keenness and versatility, it is not a good accompaniment.

Flabby consistency will make them lazy, toning down the qualities ; thus whilst they think quickly they will be slower to act.   Soft hands will make them more active than flabby ones, but not intensely so.   Elastic consistency will call out the full force of the Short-fingered qualities, and will not be so bad an addition.   Hard hands will tend to push the qualities too far.

Knotty joints reduce the quality of the quick thought and are therefore an excellent adjunct.   If only the first joint is developed, the quickness of thought will be tempered by mental order and arrangement.   If only the second Knot is developed, there will not be so much carelessness in the surroundings.

The character of the Thumb is important, for giving the determination of the large Thumb to the strong qualities of Short fingers ; but if such determination is not of the right kind, the combination will be bad.   The Clubbed Thumb would add brutal obstinacy and drive the qualities to the utmost limit.   A Flat nervous thumb will add nervous excitement.   A well-balanced thumb is required to operate on Short fingers.

The Short-fingers affect the Mounts ; the ambition, pride, religion and honour of Jupiter will have quick thought and impulse behind them.   Saturn will be less sombre, slow, mean and superstitious ; Apollo will be more brilliant ; Mercury will be rapid whether as orator, business or professional man—or thief ; Mars will need help to keep Short-fingered impetuosity from hazardous enterprises ; Luna will be less selfish and dreamy, while Venus will have the added fire of quick thought and impulse.

The Individual phalanges must be noted to see in which world the qualities will operate ; the probable outcome can then be estimated by noting whether ambition is behind them as a driving force, or whether the aggression of Mars affects them.

Above all, note the Head Line, as to whether it is strong, clear and straight, whether drooping to Luna, or if showing defects. A good clear Head line is best calculated to bring Short-fingered qualities to perfection.

They need Square tips, elastic consistency, a good thumb, a straight, clear Head Line, and then they are capable of almost any achievement. With pointed or Conic tips, hard hands, coarse or nervous thumbs, and a poor Head Line, the result can only be utter failure.

CHAPTER IV

THE THUMB AND NAILS

HAVING dealt fully with the fingers, their terminations and qualities, the Thumb now claims attention. This is by far the most important member of the hand, as without it the rest would be practically useless.

The Thumb, as in the case of the fingers, is divided into three phalanges, and the Three Worlds of Palmistry equally apply to it. These three Worlds embody three supremely important qualities, constituting the strongest moving forces in human nature, viz. :—Will power and determination, as shown by the first or nail phalanx, Reason and Logic by the second, Love and Sympathy by the third—or Mount of Venus as it is called.

The special attributes of the first phalanx are will power, decision, and the ability to command others; those of the second are perception, judgment and reasoning faculties ; those of the third, love, sympathy, and passion. A combination of these three will show an amount of moral force without which no character is strong, no brilliancy of great value.

In order to note the Thumb, have the hands held up with the palms towards you, so that you can see whether the Thumb is set high on the side of the hand, whether lwo, or in a medium position—the higher theThumb is set in the hand, the lower is the grade of intelligence, and the owner of it has less adaptability. If the Thumb is low set, the wider it will open from the side of the hand. This low set Thumb will indicate a nature full of the highest human qualities and shows generosity, a love of liberty, independence and a readiness to lend a helping hand to others. If the thumb is short, it will considerably reduce the good qualities of its low setting ; but this short low set thumb will not often be met with.

The normal length of the thumb, with medium setting, is when the tip reaches to the middle of the third phalanx of the finger of Jupiter when the thumb is held against the side of the hand.   Shorter than this, it must be judged as a short thumb.   If high set, it may reach above this standard of measurement and yet be only normal in its own length.   In noting the phalanges of the thumb, see if the first phalanx is a trifle shorter than the second—this gives the normal development.   If the Will phalanx (the first) is longer than Reason (the second), then Will is in excess of Reason and the owner will act first and think afterwards.   If Reason (the second) is longer than the Will phalanx, then Reason is in excess of Will, and whilst the owner will be good at making plans, he will not be so good in executing them—he will be a reasoner who does not act.   Do not, however, imagine that all who possess a strong Will phalanx must be successful in life ; they may have determination, even more than sufficient to push them to the front, but have they anything to push ?

A thumb placed either high, low or normally, if lying close to the side of the hand, will indicate a person who is cautious, lacking in sympathy, secretive, and hard to approach.   If with this thumb the fingers are stiff and wanting in flexibility, it enhances the peculiarities ; while if the nails are short, showing a critical nature, they will be mean and petty.

The medium setting of the thumb, not tied too closely to the side of the hand, shows a subject well balanced, not extravagant or mean, frank and open in disposition, true to friends and worth cultivating.

When the Will phalanx shows marked flexibility by the ease with which it bends back, or is seen with a decided backward inclination, it tells of extravagance, luxury, and generosity, which generally confines itself to those for whom its possessor has strong affection.   If with this indication the Mounts of Jupiter and Mars are well developed, then the extravagance will be directed to the gratification of personal vanity and display.

Persons with small thumbs are governed by the heart rather than by reason, and have far more sentiment than

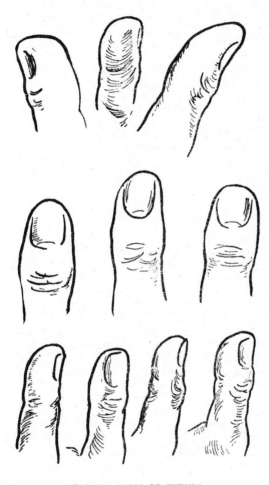

VARIOUS TYPES OF THUMBS

ideas ; large-thumbed persons are governed by the head, and are more prolific in ideas than sentiment.

Thumbs are of many shapes, and these are indicative of the personal qualities of their owners.   They are usually classified as follows :—

THE ELEMENTARY :—This is an almost shapeless thumb, and has the appearance of a piece of flesh just stuck on the hand, without any regard to symmetry, and the two joints do not show where they separate.   Its very appearance tells of heaviness, coarseness and animalism.   It is brutal in will, in reasoning, and in passion (in love), heavy, coarse, common, tactless and ignorant.   Its owner walks over every one, and is boorish and clownish even with those as coarse and common as himself.

THE NERVOUS :—This will be recognised by its flat appearance—it looks as if it had been subject to heavy pressure ; such thumbs have all kinds of tips.   As a rule they are soft and flabby, but it is the flat appearance which marks them.   This thumb shows that the nervous force, and nervous energy, are too strong for its owner. With this thumb the nails will generally be found to be fluted, there will be many lines in the hand, and a soft or flabby consistency, telling of a want of nervous balance.

THE BROAD THUMB :—This thumb is not round or shapeless as the Elementary, nor has it the flat appearance of the Nervous thumb—on the contrary, if viewed from the back, or nailed side, it has a broad look in both phalanges and bears a strong and healthy appearance. It tells of strong determination, well supported by physical strength.   It indicates the determination which succeeds, for it is pushing and aggressive, yet may easily be transformed to violent obstinacy, and often requires guidance and restraint to keep it within due bounds.

THE STRONG THUMB :—This will appear to be of equal thickness throughout its whole length, yet delicate, shapely, with Conic or Square tip.   The nail should be smooth and of good colour.   It shows strength of will, the first phalanx being good, and with sound reasoning and logical qualities, the second phalanx being equally strong.   It tells of a very diplomatic mind, firm determination, and a refined intelligent nature, yet with plenty of firmness of purpose, and gives refinement of will, intelligent reasoning, taste, tact, and perseverance.

THE PADDLE-SHAPED THUMB :—In this thumb, which is often seen, the Will phalanx is broad when looked at from the nail side, but it is not thick throughout. It is not thin or flat enough to be classed as a Nervous thumb. It shows strong determination, which, if the development is excessive, will tend to tyranny and obstinacy ; it is always a strong phalanx—even if it is deficient in length, the paddle shape gives it strength. This strength, however, is not always accompanied with robust health ; it indicates a strong mental will which, although capable of standing a heavy trial or strain, generally collapses when the strain is over.

THE FLEXIBLE THUMB :—Bends back at the joint and marks one extravagant, a spendthrift, brilliant, versatile, sentimental, generous and sympathetic, emotional and extremist. Square tips, a good Head Line, and developed Mount of Saturn are needed to give them some necessary ballast.

THE STIFF THUMB :—This carries itself erect and close to the side of the hand, and indicates the possession of a practical turn of mind, with commonsense ; economical and parsimonious. Quiet, cautious, plodding, reliable, but of a grasping nature. In estimating the force of this thumb, it will be necessary to give to it, if of fine grade, fine-grade qualities, while a coarse stiff thumb must be given coarse-grade qualities.

THE CLUBBED THUMB :—This is a thumb once seen never forgotten. It has a Will phalanx, thick and round, or broad with a short nail of coarse structure—in fact, the Will phalanx has the appearance of a badly shaped ball. Owing to its thickness, coarseness, and brutal obstinacy, this thumb has been called the "Murderer's thumb." It shows terrific obstinacy, and in a bad hand, an ungovernable temper. These coarse and disagreeable characteristics, however, may never be manifested ; they are very dangerous possessions and are generally hereditary—but in all cases it is a warning of danger of bad temper underlying, and always indicates intense obstinacy under opposition. The Knots separating the phalanges, if found, operate in practically the same way as on the fingers.

The Phalanges, next to the general shape of the thumb, must be taken into account, as well as its length. The first phalanx much longer than the second indicates a subject obstinate, tyrannical, despotic ; one who, if crossed in his plans, will fly into a temper. Where the two phalanges are equal, the qualities are balanced, and the determination will be the result of sound judgment. Firmness there will be, but it will be controlled by reason.

With the second phalanx strong and the first deficient, there will be a want of balance, and the owner will think but not act, plan but nor operate, reason but not do. With the Will phalanx very short and largely out of proportion to the second, the owner will be absolutely weak, an easy tool to any one who chooses to lead him, and easily discouraged. Thus, from excess in length of the Will phalanx to absolute deficiency, are found the various degrees of Will power, but it will be well to remember that too much is as bad as not enough.

The character of the tips must be taken into account, as they operate to increase or diminish the strength of the thumb. Conic tips make the subject impressionable, and this weakens or softens the power of the Will. The Conic qualities of impulse, love of beauty, and idealism, reduce the strength of an excessive length of the Will phalanx, and they will make it less tyrannical and despotic, and more easily influenced if the tips are Conic. On a deficient Will phalanx, the Conic tip gives hopeless weakness.

The Square tip adds strength to the deficient phalanx, commonsense to the normal one, and increases the strength of the excessive one.

The Spatulate Tip adds the spatulate qualities of independence, action and originality, and gives a commanding tone to the Will. It is a benefit to a weak phalanx, but a menace to an excessive one.

The Knots separating the phalanges, if found, operate exactly as on the fingers. It adds strength to the first phalanx, strengthens the Conic tip, and gives force to the others. It increases the reasoning of the second phalanx by lessening the intuition of the first.

A flat and flabby second phalanx denotes weakness of constitution, and want of vitality.

If the second phalanx is slender and round, the skin fine in texture, refinement in reason is indicated ; the owner will think in a refined and delicate way. If the thoughts are evil, he is more to be feared from his cleverness and adroitness, for he will be a crafty, fox-like schemer. Assuming that the thoughts are good, it is one of the best shapes.

When the second phalanx is very narrow in the middle, or waist-shaped, it indicates a brilliant tactful nature, one capable and diplomatic, and if long, of great mental strength.

GENERALLY :—Large thumbs strengthen smooth fingers, small thumbs increase the impulsiveness. Large thumbs decrease the artistic qualities of Conic and Pointed tips by making them more practical ; small thumbs make them dreamy and listless. Large thumbs drive Square or Spatulate tips to increased activity on practical lines : small thumbs make these tips mere talkers, not doers.

Large thumbs make short-fingered qualities quicker and more determined ; small thumbs decrease the practical application of the qualities. Large thumbs increase the determination of long fingers and they fully carry out the details. Long fingers and small thumbs, whilst loving details, will not trouble to receive them.

Hands with Smooth fingers, Conic or Pointed tips, and a small thumb, indicate artistic and poetic feeling.

Large hands with Knotty joints, and Square or Spatulate tips, with large thumbs, are scientific, mechanical and practical hands.

THE FINGER NAILS

A consideration of the nails is necessary, and much information as to the general health and robustness of the constitution can be obtained from them.

The nail should be smooth and pliable, but not brittle, and should be pink as to its colour. The fluting or ridging of the nail, from the top to the base, indicates nervous disorder ; if serious, there will also be a brittle condition of the nail and a marked tendency to grow away from the fingers.

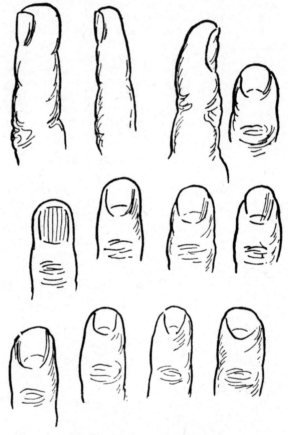

VARIOUS TYPES OF NAILS

The white flecks or spots often seen on the nails are the first indication of approaching nerve trouble ; as the disorder grows, the flecks enlarge, then coalesce, until the whole nail is clouded with them—then fluting or ridging becomes more pronounced, the nail grows brittle and begins to turn back from the end and lose its shape. At this stage there is grave danger ; the delicacy of the nerves becomes marked, and there may even be danger of paralysis.

A NARROW NAIL shows one who does not possess robust health but carries on by nervous energy. As a matter of fact, it is the Psychic nail, and the delicacy of the psychic character is present, rather than muscular health, such as is shown by the broad nail. The narrow nail may be either white, yellow, blue or pink, but never red— very often a blue colour will be seen at its base, denoting poor circulation of the blood.

THE SHORT NAIL :—This tells of a critical turn of the mind, but if not very short, it will be more of the nature of investigation. The extremely short nail, flat, with the skin growing on it, shows pugnacity and an argumentative disposition. Add to this nail knotty fingers, a big thumb and hard hands, with the Mounts of Mars well developed, and a most pugnacious and disagreeable person will be the result.

OPEN AND FRANK NAILS :—These are broad at the tip, curve round the finger, broadening at the base and pink in colour. They reveal a nature open and frank, to whom honesty of thought is natural. They are broad open-looking nails, and their breadth shows the broad views and ideas of their owners—this is especially so if they are pink in colour.

SQUARE-ENDED NAILS :—These taper towards the base, and are often seen on long fingers—this is an indication of heart trouble, and these nails are found on all shapes of fingers or hands ; the nail is small and often of a deep blue colour at the base, and shows structural weakness of the heart.

BULBOUS NAIL :—This is so pronounced in its shape, that, once seen, it can never be forgotten. The end of the finger as well as the nail has to be taken in conjunction with it. It may be and is seen on any tip, but whenever seen it will show an advanced stage of consumption or tubercular trouble.   Often the colour will be blue, show-ing interference with the circulation.

THE CURVED NAIL has somewhat the appearance of the bulbous nail, but it is not the same ; it is always a large nail and may be found on any shaped tip—it is the curving or semi-bulbous formation which marks it.   It shows delicacy of the throat and bronchial tubes, and tells of one very susceptible to colds.   Its indications will be con-firmed by Islands on the Line of Mercury.   This curved nail is often found on the feet.

The colour under the nails must be carefully noted.   The white nail shows a natural coldness of disposition.   The yellow colour seen under some nails will tell of bile in the blood.   Redness shows intense ardour and strength. The blue indicates, as I have before remarked, a want of circulation.

CHAPTER V

THE Mounts are seven in number, and of these four are located at the base of the fingers, two on the side of the hand, on what is termed the percussion, and one at the base of the thumb, which properly constitutes the third phalanx of the thumb. These Mounts are especially valuable in determining the type to which a subject belongs, without which the clearest and most accurate delineation cannot be given.

Each of the fingers is named after the Mount to which it is attached, and partakes of the qualities of its particular Mount. As each Mount represents one of the original types into which the human race was divided, it is only from a due consideration of the development of some one or more of the Mounts that the type of the subject can be obtained.

They vary in appearance in the hands, for in some cases they form little hills under the fingers, while in other hands they are so flat as to be almost indistinguishable on the palm—indeed, in some hands, where the Mounts should be seen, there are only depressions or hollows. The Mounts which are very prominent in the hand are what are termed Strong Mounts, those which are flat are ordinary, while in the hands where there are depressions the Mount qualities are wanting.

The first aim in examining the Mounts will be to find which is the strongest one. Whichever it may be, it will show that the qualities of that Mount type are the leading ones. When one Mount is seen large and the others only normal, and on this Mount is a single deep vertical line, while the finger of the Mount is very long and well developed, it will indicate one who is practically a pure specimen of the type represented by the Mount. In order-however, to judge the extent to which the qualities of this strong Mount will operate, the Mount must not be flabby and its colour should be warm.

It is not often that a hand is seen with only one Mount developed ; sometimes the hand will have two Mounts equally developed, and in such cases there will be a combination of the two types represented by the Mount. To ascertain which is the stronger of these Mounts, if one of them has a deep vertical line on it, or should be harder or redder than the other, this will show it to be the leading Mount.

Failing these indications, then the length and character of the fingers must be noted to ascertain their capability of increasing the strength or otherwise of the Mounts. The normal length of the finger of Jupiter should be to the middle of the first phalanx of the finger of Saturn—this latter should always be longer than the others in order to give balance to the character.   The finger of Apollo should also reach to the middle of the first phalanx of Saturn, and the finger of Mercury should reach the first Knot of Apollo.   If it is longer than this, the Mercurian qualities will be very pronounced ; if shorter than the Knot, the Mercurian qualities will be deficient.

When all the Mounts seem to be equally balanced, the character will be a well-balanced one, combining the qualities of all the types, and the life should be generally tranquil and happy, provided the Mounts are without defects.

All the Mounts have their bad side as well as the good, and in deciding which side is the stronger, recourse must be had to the markings on the Mounts.   As a general rule, it is found that Vertical lines are good, whilst Horizontal lines which cut them are bad—this crossing of the Vertical and Horizontal lines is termed a Grille, and constitutes a defect of the Mount on which it is seen.

Some of the Mount types are more inclined to be evil than others, hence it will be necessary to note the markings on the Mounts, the colour and Nails, as they will tell whether the defects are of the health or character. It will be necessary to examine both hands, comparing them to ascertain whether the course of the life has been progressive or retrograde.

In all cases, the character of the fingers—whether they are long or short, smooth or knotty—and the class of tips must be studied in connection with the Mount qualities and the health troubles incidental thereto, as well as the nails.

THE MOUNT OF JUPITER

This Mount is situated at the base of the first or Index finger, to which it gives the name Jupiter, and is seen, of course, on both hands. The method of judging the Mounts, in order to determine which is the strongest, has already been detailed, as also the way to proceed when several Mounts are equally well developed.

The Jupiterian is always ambitious and a leader amongst men. He is to be found in all the walks of life. He is to be found in politics, the army, and the church. Religion is a strong feature with the Jupiterian, but he will be found holding all shades of opinion, from the ultra-ortho-dox to a line close to scepticism—the tip of the finger of Jupiter will tell you to which extreme he leans. Ambi-tion, love of command, pride of position, religion, love of nature, and a love of ceremony and display, are his pre-dominant characteristics. The type is a good and strong one, but a pure Jupiterian is not frequently met with, as there is generally an admixture of other types.

The pure Jupiterian is of medium height, strongly built and inclined to be fleshy; the skin is smooth and clear, generally fine in texture, healthy-looking and pink in colour ; the eyes large and expressive, particularly when under emotion. The nose is straight, well formed, tending to be large and often Roman in shape, the mouth large, with lips full and red. The cheeks are well rounded and full, the chin long and firm and with a dimple at the point ; the hair is usually brown, often running to chest-nut. The constitution is strong and vigorous.

The personality of the Jupiterian is well calculated to command followers, and he is not without a good measure of vanity in his composition, but he is always kind-hearted and sympathetic, as well as generous. Always dashing and extravagant. Power and rule mean far more to him than money, and though through his enterprises he may make large amounts, he does not hoard.

Religion is natural to him, but being a lover of show and ceremony, in his mode of worship, his forms of government, anywhere and everywhere, he will glory in pageantry and observance of form. Prefers peace to war, hence he is a strong believer in law and order, and a seeker for popularity. Being naturally honest, he despises dishonesty and fraud. The strong feature of the type is ambition, and with this to stimulate the strong qualities, it is small wonder that the Jupiterian is the most invincible of the types.

To sum up the leading characteristics of Jupiter, they will be found to be :—Ambition, religion, honour, leadership, pride, dignity, and the love of nature. The Jupiterian in respect to marriage is very ambitious ; he usually marries young, choosing one of whom he can be proud—but like many others, he often finds himself unhappy in his married life.

As regards health, he is liable to certain complaints. Not only is he a great eater, but he is partial to high living, and may in consequence suffer from over-eating. This injures the digestive organs and renders him liable to vertigo and fainting fits, as a warning—such attacks increase in severity, if the over-indulgence is continued, until apoplexy ends his career. He is also liable to gout and stomach troubles, which produce impurity of the blood, often affecting the lungs.

Having definitely settled your subject as a Jupiterian, the hand considered as a whole will reveal the plane on which he will function. With the mental world strongest, his ambition will lead him to adopt a literary career ; if the middle, or material, world is strongest, he will seek to lead in business or commercial concerns ; if the lower third is strongest, being already a sensual person, he will become more sensual and bad results will follow.

The best combination of the Worlds is that of the two upper ones ; the next would be that of the two lower ones, for in this case the commonsense of the middle one would hold the lower in check ; but given a combination of the

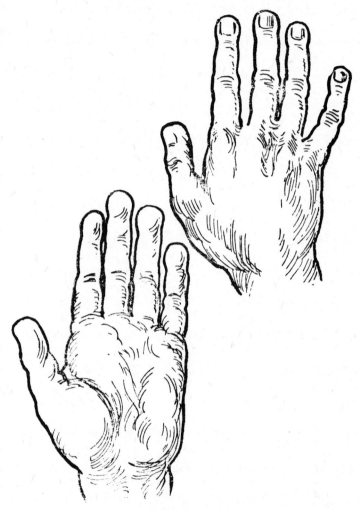

SPATULATE TIPS, WITH STRONG MOUNT OF JUPITER

first and third worlds, the result would be a sensual dreamer.

This system of combination also applies to the individual fingers, but especially so to the finger of Jupiter. By noting which phalanx of the finger of Jupiter is longest, you will easily ascertain which world is predominant if a long finger is seen, and also which is shortest with a short finger.

If the finger of Jupiter reaches to the centre of the first phalanx of the finger of Saturn, the desire for leadership will not be excessive ; if it is as long as Saturn, the desire for domination will be strong, and if longer than Saturn it will indicate the absolute tyrant. If, however, it is shorter than the first joint of Saturn, the subject will not be a pure Jupiterian, even though the Mount is a strong one, as the essential element of leadership will be absent.

If the first phalanx (which indicates mental strength) is long, then that World will rule, and religion and intuition will be strong ; with Conic tips, idealistic and intuitive qualities will be added to the mental. With a Square tip, there will be more of the commonsense, regularity and order, and less will be taken for granted. With a Spatulate tip there will be more originality in his views and actions. The excessively Square or Spatulate tip indicates a domineering spirit, which, in family, business and general affairs of life, amounts to despotism and tyranny. The broader this first phalanx, the more domineering and the less religious will the subject be.

The second phalanx tells of the business side of the Jupiterian, and of the ambition which operates as a driving force. If this is long, then the practical affairs of life will take his attention, as he will aim for leadership in the business world. Again we must apply the tip qualities, but with a strong second phalanx, Square tips make the best accompaniment. Spatulate tips would show an active, ambitious and original person, who will force his way in the world, on practical lines—the Conic tip, adding the conic quality of idealism, would not be so good.

By far the most important phalanx to notice is the third, as to its length and thickness—whether it is long and thick, whether long and waist-like, or whether short, with any of these combinations.

If it is only long but not thick, it will indicate that the qualities of the lower world are normal in their influence, assisting and supporting the upper phalanges. If the length of this third phalange should exceed the other two, it would indicate that ambition and desire to rule would be sordid, and would operate in a manner not always refined. The whole nature would be coarse, but sensualism would not be present as the phalanx is not thick ; if long and thick, then gluttony must be added, with a corresponding liability to the health troubles of the type, especially apoplexy. In the long and waist-like third phalanx we have the gluttony absent ; the aims and ideals of the subject will be of a higher nature ; with this waist-like phalanx the gluttony common to Jupiterians will be absent, and the usual health difficulties will also be absent—the health troubles likely to arise will be from the lungs and throat, or nervousness.

A Cross on the Mount is commonly held to indicate a happy marriage, and if there is also a Star on the Mount a brilliant alliance. In practice, however, I have but once been able to verify this as correct. In my opinion the Star really indicates gratified ambition in some direction— which may, or may not be marriage.

In dealing with the Mount of Jupiter, and in fact with all the finger Mounts, the general chierognomatic characteristics of the respective fingers and their qualities must be applied, as affecting the operations of the Mount.

THE MOUNT OF SATURN

This Mount is situated at the base of the second finger. The higher this Mount is developed and the longer and larger the finger, the more clearly pronounced is the type of the subject. A highly developed Mount of Saturn is not often found, and in the majority of hands there is a depression. The long finger of Saturn is frequently seen, indicating the possession of *some* of the Saturnian qualities.

Generally speaking, the Saturnian may be recognised by the straight upright finger of Saturn, with the other fingers leaning towards it.

The Saturnian is a peculiar person, always fastidious and particular even as regards trifles, prudent and wise ; but if the development is excessive, he would be a veritable wet-blanket to damp enthusiasm—his point of view is the gloomy one, and he is ever ready to bring it forward.   To bring out its best side, the development should be slight.

He is the tallest of the types, and the representative finger is the largest on the hand.   Gaunt, thin and pale, the skin is yellow and wrinkled.   His hair is dark, often black, thick but straight and harsh, often losing it while young.   The face is long and thin, with high cheek bones. The eyebrows are thick, the eyes deep-set and black, with a gloomy expression, changing only when anger or excitement stirs him.   The nose is long, straight and thin, with pointed end.   The mouth is large, with thin pale lips, the lower jaw prominent.   The chest is thin, the shoulders high with a decided stoop, whilst the arms are long and hang lifelessly at his sides.   The whole appearance of the typical Saturnian is that of one who sees no bright side to life ; he is wanting in vitality, warmth and attractiveness.

He is cynical, devoid of veneration, and ever the doubter. Very unsocial, and does not seek the companionship of others, but is, as a rule, an ardent student, with a liking for chemistry, and is often proficient in occultism.   Cautious and prudent.   Mistrustful of all, he rarely goes into business enterprises with others.   In investments he prefers land, farms and houses, as less speculative than stocks and shares, bonds or mercantile enterprises.   He is very hard to get on with, for he always looks on the dark side of things and is timid and nervous.

He is not one who cares to marry, and in regard to this question very strong indications must be present before venturing a prediction.   Very self-reliant, independent, and cares little for the opinion of others.

The prudence which marks him gives him another trait—he is saving, even mean and miserly, and the more strongly the Saturnian indications are marked, the stronger will be the avaricious tendencies.   He is very musical and is often a fine performer and a composer, but his music will be severely classical and often tinged with sadness.

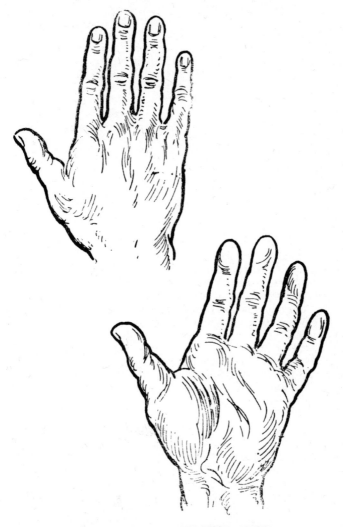

SQUARE TIPS WITH STRONG SECOND FINGER

With the Mount of Saturn badly grilled, or with crossed developments of the Mount, a bad Heart Line, with crooked fingers and a hard hand, the type will be a bad one.

With respect to health, the Saturnian is a purely bilious type, and as the presence of the bile in the blood creates nervous conditions, this may be looked for and an examination of the nails will show its extent. Rheumatism, hemorrhoids and varicose veins may trouble him. Paralysis is also one of his dangers. Delicate teeth, and ear troubles are not unusual. These health troubles, if present, will be found on the Life Line. The Grille or Cross-bars on the Mount will suggest their presence, while the nature of the trouble can be ascertained from the nails and so on.

This Mount must be handled carefully, as the type is a peculiar one, and it will be essential to ascertain to what extent the subject may be affected by other and redeeming qualities.

A measure of Saturnian should be present, as otherwise there would be a want of balance in the character. Excess would result in morbidity, gloom, melancholy and pessimism. Hence all the cheirognomic tests must be applied, and the hand as a whole considered, for given the fingers in excess of the palm, the mental world will predominate. This will indicate the student and scholar, who will write books or make a good teacher, but would not be a success in business. Given the middle portion of the hand in excess, you have the business man ; if the lower portion of the hand is most strongly developed, then the grosser qualities will be manifest. Should one of the three Worlds be absent while the other two are developed, the effect of the combination must be worked out—thus, should the upper and lower worlds be strong, with the middle world absent, you will have a subject not only visionary, but ruled by bad material motives, unrestrained—bear in mind, however, that the Saturnian is not a sensualist.

Apply also to this Mount the Worlds as read from the phalanges of the fingers. The first being longest indicates that the mental world leads, and will reveal the student, inclined to be superstitious, with a love of occult studies. The second phalanx being the longest indicates that the business side will lead, and that farming, chemistry, mining, scientific research, history and mathematics, will be vocations most to his taste. If the third phalanx is strongest, then the baser qualities will predominate— especially if this phalanx is thick and the hand coarse or bad, when the miser will be seen. If it is waist-like, the desire for study will be most marked. The finger being bent will give added shrewdness to the Saturnian qualities. Should the finger be short, the subject is not a Saturnian and is utterly wanting in seriousness and balance.

Generally apply all the cheirognomic tests, and bear in mind that although the Saturnian is always more or less gloomy by nature, and predisposed to suicide under a strong sense of ill-success, sickness or slight, yet if he is of a high type, he may by mental force hold himself level. Do not run away with the idea that all Saturnians are bad. Some of the noblest, most high-minded and successful of men have belonged to this type—as well as some of the most depraved and vicious.

The combination of this Mount with a prominent Mount of Jupiter will give patience and respect ; with a strong Mercury there will be a love of Medicine and a desire for knowledge. In combination with Venus, it will give a love of truth in occultism, charity and self-control. In every case a strong Mount of Saturn indicates a love of music, and will generally be seen strongly marked amongst composers.

THE MOUNT OF APOLLO

This Mount is situated at the base of the third finger, in conjunction with which it serves to mark out the Apollonian type of individual, and it is one of the pleasantest types to handle.

As a rule, the Apollonian is healthy, happy and genial, strongly artistic, and with him the darker side of life is always in the background. He not only looks to the bright side, but endeavours to make others do so as well, and thus helps to make life worth living.

It must, however, be remembered that although a lover of the beautiful and artistic, he is not necessarily a creator of them—which is quite another thing. Before predicting the possession of *creative* artistic powers, a long finger of Apollo, with the first phalanx long, and a good deep Line of Apollo, often with Stars on it, will be essential.

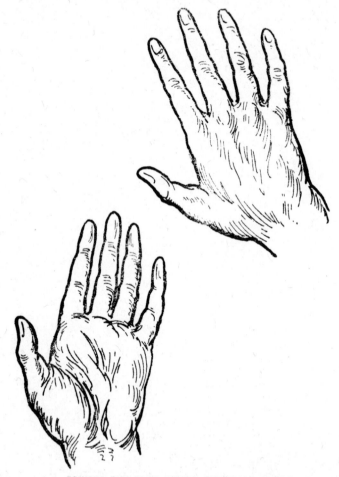

POINTED TIPS WITH STRONG FINGER OF APOLLO

The Apollonian possesses also a business side, and in this he is often successful, though his love of beauty will probably be displayed in it.   Attractive, with a readiness of adaption to existing conditions and the needs of the public, he lays himself out to attract and please—and success follows.   This Apollonian will possess a high Mount, but not necessarily with deep lines—if these are seen, there will generally be several vertical lines, giving diversity of talent.   As a rule you will also see a well developed Mount of Mercury, giving business shrewdness.

He is of medium height, graceful, athletic and supple, with a clear complexion and healthy.   Highly intuitive, often inventive, he sees through things quickly, and this faculty is particularly strong in literature and art.   Being often inventive, he is good at imitation, and often gets credit for much greater knowledge than he possesses— owing to his versatility, he will be able to pass muster in whatever society he may be found.   He is invariably cheerful and happy, but has a quick fierce temper when roused ; he is not one to harbour animosity or resentment, nor is he one to make lasting friendships.   He does not therefore inspire lasting friendship in others.

The good type Apollonian, though a lover of pleasure, is neither amorous nor sensual ; he does not indulge in dissipation, but is a great traveller.   Predisposed to marry, yet generally he is most unfortunate in his matrimonial ventures.

Of course there are bad Apollonians.   The Mount and finger will be strong enough to show that the subject belongs to the type, but the short first phalanx and thick third, with short nails and crooked finger, will show a want of the fineness of the type, and indicate one who is vain, boastful, with a good opinion of himself, fond of show and display, with all the extravagance of the type without the capacity to make money.   Craving notoriety and overestimtaing himself, he becomes a man with a grievance and at variance with all.   Of course there are many degrees of development between the good and the bad type, and there will often be found a combination with other types, which must be considered in judging the measure of Apollonian qualities possessed.

Naturally this type is a healthy one, yet it has its difficulties, and Heart trouble is the principal one. The nails must be noted, the Heart Line also for islands, cross-bars, stars or other defects, and the Life Line for signs of delicacy marked thereon, while there may be a grille on the Mount itself. Eye-weakness is another of the type troubles, which is indicated by a small dot or Island on the Head Line under the Mount. Fevers are likely, but they will be acute attacks.

The Hand as a whole must be noted, as it will tell in which World the subject will move. Should the fingers reach beyond the palm, then the mind will be the ruling factor, and the subject will in all probability find his sphere of action in literature, art, poetry, drawing, or subjects of a similar nature. Given the middle world the strongest, then business will claim him. If the lower world is the strongest, and the third phalanx of the finger of Apollo is thick, then the beast instincts will prevail.

If the Mounts of Apollo and Mercury are equally developed, it will give one in whom justice, decision, and a love of scientific research are the predominant characteristics, while if the middle world predominates, it will give added shrewdness in business affairs. Combined with Mount Luna, there will be commonsense, imagination, a love of travel, reflection, and a measure of gaiety. Combined with Mount Venus, the amiability and desire to please will be increased.

If the Mount is absent in both hands, there will be an utter indifference to art, and the trend of the life will be dull, unenlightened and monotonous.

For the best results of the type, there should be smooth fingers with mixed tips, a strong second phalanx to the thumb, with one or three good lines on the Mount, but preferably one deep clear line only.

THE MOUNT OF MERCURY

This Mount is situated at the base of the fourth finger, and in conjunction with it, marks the Mercurian, whose varied capabilities will necessitate careful consideration.

The first essential, with this type, is to find out which

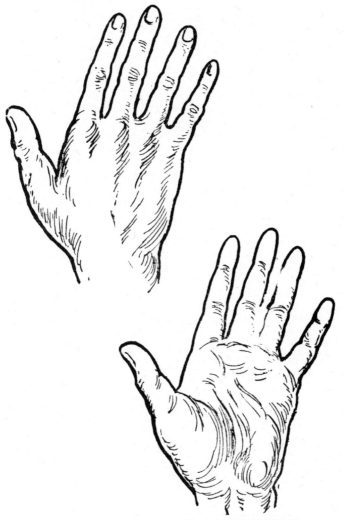

POINTED OR CONIC FINGERS WITH DOMINANT MERCURY

side, the good or the bad, is the stronger, for of all the types the Mercurian is most easily led into dishonest practice. If good, the Mercurian is one of the best, and most successful in science, eloquence, industry, law, politics or medicine ; on the other hand, no greater cheats, swindlers or liars can be found.

The Mercurian is of medium height, very compact in build, neat in his appearance, and with an expressive countenance, always conveying a sense of restless activity —as a rule, he retains a more or less youthful appearance in old age.

He is the most active of all the types, both physically and mentally. Proficient in all games and athletic sports, where skill and dexterity rather than physical strength are needed. Possessing as he does good powers of expression, he will be quite at home in debate or argument, and aided by his quick intuition he comes out ahead on his side of the question.

He is keen on scientific study and a born mathematician. In the medical profession he is generally successful, especially so if the Mount is marked by three vertical lines, with a well-developed Mount of Jupiter to lend strong ambition as a driving force to his natural energy, scientific aptitudes and keenness.

In the practice of the law, given a long pointed first phalanx to the finger and short nails, he will make his mark as a Barrister. He is also a close student of the occult sciences, and in the ranks of those who are interested in the occult you will find Mercurians. If a badly marked Mount, with crooked finger, is shown, you will find not only the untrue Clairvoyant, but the Palmist who will tell you not only your own name but the names of your friends! As a matter of experience and fact, those who thus glibly under take the impossible are specimens of the bad type of Mercurian.

Mercurians are keen in business and shrewd, are excellent actors and mimics, and on the good side they are not vicious, though generally keen and shrewd. They are fond of children and like having them around them, so long as they do not interfere with their other employments. They are versatile and often try a variety of occupations, and are apt to be envious of the success of others. As a rule they marry early and are fond of home life.

The type is a healthy one, though somewhat bilious and of a decidedly nervous temperament ; stomach trouble, dyspepsia and similar troubles may affect him. This bilious trend of the type produces a class who, by their practices, are more deserving of being put into prison than many already there—the demarcation line between business shrewdness and actual dishonesty is easily passed, and once over the boundary their customers are cheated wholesale. These unscrupulous traders may possess nice-looking hands, but close observation will disclose the crooked finger of Mercury, while an inspection of their hands would reveal cross-bars on the Mount, or a grille with narrow quadrangles. Such an inspection will not be easy, as instinctively they hide their hands, or wash them with invisible soap—there is nothing open-handed about them. They are dishonest, no matter in what state of life they may move. The crooked finger, and grilled or cross-barred Mount, mark them as subject to continued temptation to dishonesty.

The actually criminal Mercurian may be small in stature, with shiftless restless eyes, but he or she will be marked out by the crooked, gnarled fingers, twisted, and bent towards the palm, a grilled Mount, a defective or absent Heart Line, high stiff thumb—amongst such, you have the criminal pure and simple.

Thus in dealing with a Mercurian you must grade him and note what are the underlying forces. The whole of the hand will tell you this; the rules must be carefully applied and the influence of the other Mounts must be calculated. Thus, a well-developed Mount of Saturn will help, but as a rule the Mount of Mercury is not often found in combination with other Mounts. The absence of the Mount would indicate incapacity for either commercial or scientific undertakings.

In dealing with this type, the finger must be considered,

strongly Mercurian. Note which phalanx is longest, for it is with this type that the three Worlds of Palmistry are most strongly evidenced. The first phalanx long gives great powers of expression, even to eloquence and oratory —especially is this so if the finger has a pointed tip. The second phalanx being longest, the scientific side of the type will be most marked, and law, medicine or science is indicated. Given the third phalanx the longest, then commerce will be the occupation, and the business man or merchant is shown. The tips must be noted and the respective qualities of the class to which it belongs must be applied.

The best marking on the Mount, either singly or in combination, are the single vertical line, star, square, triangle, or trident. On the other hand, the grille, island, cross, dot or cross-bars show the bad qualities of the Mount, either as to health or character, which you can determine by the nails.

THE MOUNT OF MARS

This Mount is of a three-fold nature, and consists of the Mount of Mars properly so called, situated under the Mount of Mercury, between the Heart and Head Lines and designated the Upper Mars ; the Lower Mars, situated between the Life Line and Mount Venus ; and the Plain of Mars, which constitutes the centre of the palm. Each has its special influence, making this Mount a difficult one to comprehend, while the difficulty is enhanced because there is no finger representing the Mount.

The leading characteristics of the Mount when well developed are courage, self-control, resolution, and capability for command. In almost all hands some Martian development is to be found—to its entire absence is due the flotsam and jetsam of life. Easily discouraged, they go under in the struggle for existence, no matter how gifted or talented they may be.

There are two kinds of fighters—those who are aggressive and force the issue, and those who act purely on the defensive. This division in the Martian qualities is revealed in the Upper Mount of Mars, which indicates *resistive power*, and the Lower Mount of Mars, which indicates the possession of *aggressive power*. The degree of development of these Mounts varies—often one of these Mounts only is strongly developed, while the other is small ; in such case the subject will either be very aggressive, or have strong resistive power, according to the more strongly developed Mount.

Given both Mounts well developed, you have one possessed of strong aggressive and resistive powers ; one who will have much persistence, and will resist any attempts to impose on him. Such a subject will push himself over every obstacle, and resist any and every attempt to retard his progress. He will never recognise defeat when it comes.

The Plain of Mars, if well developed, or if crossed with many fine lines, will show the presence of sudden temper. With this indication, both Mounts being well developed, the combination is dangerous.

When reading hands, this Mount must be fully considered and taken into account in all its aspects ; for if deficient, there will be a want of fighting or resistive power, and failure must result—in almost all cases of suicide, this Mount will be found to be deficient.

The subject with the Upper Mount only developed will not be the one to force a fight, nor to look for trouble ; but he will resist opposition. The Lower Mount developed will show one who will not consider others, but will force his way through all opposition—he loves a fight. If, however, the Lower Mount is strong and the Upper Mount absent, your subject will be good for a game of bluff—but will back down if pressed ; he is wanting in powers of resistance.

The Martian is of medium height, strongly built, very exact, and has all the appearance of one able to look after himself, and force his way through the world—mentally if he can, physically if he must. His health is, as a rule, good, hence he is always energetic. Generous and fond of forming friendships with congenial spirits. Very determined, but amenable to reason ; fairly easily led, but to drive him would be a task for a Hercules—intense in everything and passionate, opposition will arouse his fighting propensities : he is best handled by tact and diplomacy. The type will be found in every walk of life, and is always the same ardent, persevering individual, strong in pride, and fond of show.

Naturally enough, there is a bad type of Martian as well as a good one, then you will find him lascivious, a drunkard and a criminal. To distinguish the varied degrees of the Martian, regard must be had to the various qualities of the hand as to texture, consistency, colour, and so on, in order to form a just and accurate estimate of the subject.

It must be borne in mind that the cross-lines, grilles, crosses or stars in the Plain of Mars make the subject more easily inflammable.

MOUNT LUNA

The qualities of this Mount are to a greater or lesser degree found in nearly all subjects ; but it is not often seen in its fullest development, and its strength must be judged by its curve outwardly, on the percussion of the hand, and the size of the pad it forms on the palm. If it forms a well-defined bulge on the percussion, it must be considered as being *well developed*. If it is also thick, and forms a large pad on the palm, then it must be considered as *very strongly developed* ; while if the bulge is very large, and the pad in the palm equally marked, then the development will be *excessive*.

When considering this Mount, it must be borne in mind that Vertical lines add to the strength of the Mount, while Horizontal lines indicate defects.

For health purposes, the Mount should be divided into three sections, viz. : the upper, the middle, and the lower ; each section serves to indicate the health troubles peculiar to the Lunarian, and they are indicated by crosses, grilles, cross-bars, islands, dots, ill-formed stars and wavy lines.

In a subject possessing a well-developed Mount of Luna you have one with good powers of expression, and with a pleasing and lively imagination—thus all great linguists, writers of fiction or romance, as well as musicians, possess a well-developed Mount of Luna. Where there is an excessive development of the Mount there will be flightiness, too strong an imagination, a probability (under excitement) of complete loss of control and even a danger of insanity. A deficiency of the Mount leads to a total want of imagination, a disbelief in everything, want of nerve, a hopeless outlook and hypochondria.

The Lunarian is often peculiar, especially where the Mount is well developed ; being influenced by the imagination, he becomes dreamy, builds castles in the air, conlceives great enterprises of no practical utility. Often imagines he is ill, is fickle, changeable and restless, hence he frequently becomes a great traveller. The more the Mount is lined, the more restless he becomes. He is a great believer in the superstitious, in signs and omens which influence him greatly. He loves music and prefers the classical ; is often a composer, or if the type is mental, he becomes a writer of fiction or romance, some even of history—but he will be much aided by the possession of a ong finger of Mercury, with the first phalanxe long, and the qualities of the conic, spatulate or square tip. He is very fond of the water and makes a good sailor ; he is never generous—is lacking in self-confidence, energy and perseverance, and is usually unsuccessful in business.

Fortunately the *pure* Lunarian is not often met—otherwise there would be a need for more lunatic asylums ; but the development of the Mount must be *very excessive* before attributing such a result to your subject.

This type is subject to many health troubles ; he is prediposed to gout and rheumatism, and intestinal troubles of all descriptions—in my experience I have found that intestinal disorder for *any type* is shown on the upper part of this Mount by dots, islands, cross-bars or similar defective markings ; when such are seen the Life Line should be examined closely for defects. Hair lines may often be seen running from such markings on the Mount to the Life Line, and if the Line is defective, the date of the occurrence of the trouble will be indicated—the Line of Mercury will also have to be considered, and the Mount of Saturn.

The middle portion of the Mount, if defective, will show the indications for gout or rheumatism. The lower part of the Mount with defective markings will show liability to kidney and bladder trouble in a man's hand, while in a woman's hand it will in addition indicate marked female weakness. I have found that kidney trouble is most often shown by cross-bars on the lower part of the Mount. In the case of female weakness being indicated, there is usually a Star on the Line of Mercury at the point where it crosses the Head Line. When such is seen, it is a serious indication, for its presence is indicative of sterility, and serves to explain why apparently healthy women are childless.

Bear in mind that these defective markings are not restricted in their indications to pure Lunarians; they will be found in all types, but in the hand of a Lunarian, who is peculiarly liable to such troubles, the effect of the defective marking is accentuated.

The Lunarian, as in all other types, has a bad as well as a good side, and when the bad side is developed, you will have a person who is talkative, and who, by excess of imagination, will deceive himself and others. He is mean, cowardly, selfish, insolent, deceitful, slanderous, and by no means an agreeable or pleasant companion.

In all cases of a strongly developed Mount of Luna, the qualities indicated by the other parts of the hand will exercise a strong influence ; particularly the texture of the skin, as this will indicate the amount of fineness or coarseness to be taken into account. The medium texture best suits the Lunarian, as it tells of energy and practical ideas—the consistency of the hand must be noted and its flexibility, so that you can add the varied characteristics thereto pertaining.

The pure Lunarian ranges from the highly gifted to the insane, and all the stages are indicated by the size, character, and markings of the Mount. In the absence of the Mount, you would have dense materialism. You will not find many typical Lunarians, but you may confidently expect to discover a measure of Lunarian qualities in most subjects.

THE MOUNT OF VENUS

The Venusian type is the pleasantest to meet, being healthy, happy, musical and joyous, and though, at times, it may descend in morality, it is always attractive and agreeable. It is a type which needs to be handled carefully if you are to estimate it correctly ; otherwise serious mistakes in character may be made, and low desires and practices attributed to one whose domain in iife may belong to the elevated Venusian type.

The Mount stands for love, sympathy and generosity ; the type is a good one, as one of its best qualifications is to be found in its attractiveness. It is a healthy type and a handsome one, as well as being essentially a feminine one, and is beset by many temptations from its attractiveness to the opposite sex. A good Head Line and a strong Thumb are necessary to restrain the inclinations and the passions.

A strong Mount of Venus in a woman's hand will not tend to profligacy as a Mount of the same strength would in a man's hand. In a man's hand, a strong Mount of Venus makes him either effeminate in his characteristics, or else fiery and heated in his passions. In conjunction with a hard hand, the desires will be indulged to a far greater extent than in the case of a woman with the same degree of development.

If the Mount is full and smooth, there will be a strong love of all Venusian things ; but this will not be in excess as would be the case if the Mount was grilled. Smooth Mounts, not large, indicate a love of flowers, music dancing, paintings, colour, and so on, but not strong sexual passion. If on the Mount the cross-lines constituting the grille are deep and red, it will add to the danger of the Mount.

The Venusians are honest and truthful—they are not schemers for money-making and are not given to pettifogging cheating in business. Music always appeals powerfully to them, and wherever a well developed Mount is possessed, there will be found a love of music and particularly of melody. If Mount Luna is equally developed, it will add to the musical taste of the subject.

Venusians always marry and generally at an early age ; to them the Martian strength and vigour is an attraction. Good health is their normal condition ; there are no recognised chronic ailments peculiar to the type, hence the diseases that a Venusian may have must be looked for on the other Mounts, and not on the Mount of Venus itself.

Bad Venusians there are, and they may be recognised by the hand being very thick, especially the base of the hand and the third phalanges of the fingers, the Mount of Venus being large, red and hard ; with the fingers smooth, short, and the first phalanges also short, we have mere animals, who find their pleasures only in pandering to their animal passions.

In considering the extent and power of the qualities of the Mount, and their effect upon the subject, the examination must be close and minute as to texture of the skin, the consistency of the hands, the tips of the fingers, whether long or short, knotty or smooth, the strength or otherwise of the Thumb and Head Line, and the colour of the hands—all should be brought into consideration. The other Mounts must also be considered in order to ascertain which type is secondary to it, for whatever such type may be, it must be considered as a driving power to the Venusian.

The Apollonian too closely resembles the Venusian to constitute a good combination. The Lunarian is by no means a good secondary force ; for imagination being strong, it would tend to inflame the passions. To round off and perfect the Venusian, some side of the Jupiterian, Saturnian, Mercurian or Martian type is requisite. As regards the finger tips—which exercise a strong influence on the Venusian—the Spatulate tip makes a good combination with the Mount, as it would make the subject more human in sympathy and love, very fond of pets, children, dogs, horses, and in fact all animals.

Of the whole of the seven pure types, the brightest, the best, and the most human, is without doubt the Venusian ; but whilst recognising its good qualities, it cannot be proclaimed as faultless.

In dealing with the Mounts, the opening sections of Chapter V must be considered, as they will serve to show the influence the Mounts exercise on the character and life of the subject—especially in hands which show two or more Mounts developed, as they must then be considered in combination, and in such consideration much that would otherwise appear obscure or even puzzling in the subject will be revealed.

GENERAL MOUNT INDICATIONS

Each Mount has its good and its bad side—a strong and a weak side. Well developed and well placed, it shows the good side ; grilled and cross-lined or with cross-bars, islands and crosses, the defects are uppermost.

In some hands the Mounts may be seen all equally developed. This will indicate a well-balanced character, and a general supply of qualities derived from all the types. Such subjects will be even-tempered, broad in their views and amenable to reason. If two Mounts only are developed, the subject will be a combination of the two. In this case if one Mount has a good vertical line, or is harder or redder in colour, then this Mount will be the stronger of the two.

If unable, by this method, to ascertain which is the leading type, then note the fingers carefully—for the Mount with the strongest finger will lead.

In all cases the character of the fingers, whether long or short, smooth or knotty, and the class of the tip, must be applied in connection with the Mount qualities and the diseases incidental thereto. But in a search for defects, the nails must be noted, as they disclose defects of health and character.

On many hands it will be found that the Mounts bear divers markings, all bearing on the health or character of the subject. For the benefit of my readers I give the following indications of such signs and the health defects of the particular Type.

Jupiter :—The Star, Circle, Triangle, Square, Trident and Single Vertical line add strength to the Mount ; whilst the Grille, Cross-bar, Island, Horizontal line, Dot or Cross indicate defects of health or character, which the Main lines, Colour, and so on, will determine. The Signs may be single or in combination.

Health troubles peculiar to the Type include over-eating, fainting fits, apoplexy, gout, stomach troubles, sometimes lung troubles, dyspepsia, and if the Third phalanx of the finger is waisted, nervousness, and throat or lung trouble. If the third phalanx is flabby, but shows evidence of having been thick and firm, it will indicate dyspepsia.

Saturn :—The signs either single or in combination which add strength to this Mount are the Triangle, Trident, Circle, Square, or Single Vertical line. The Grille, Cross, Island, or Cross-bars indicate defects.

Health troubles include biliousness, rheumatism, nerves, hæmorrhoids, varicose veins, ear troubles, and predisposition to suicidal pessimism.

Apollo :—The signs either single or in combination which add strength to this Mount are the Star, Triangle, Square, Trident, or Single Vertical line. The Grille, Cross, Island, Dot, or Cross-bars show defects in either health or character.

Health troubles :—weak eyes, heart trouble, sunstroke, fever.

Mercury :—The signs either single or in combination which add strength to this Mount are the Triangle, Star, Circle, Trident, Square, or Single Vertical line. The Grille, Island, Cross-bars, or Dot show the defects of the Mount, in either health or character.

Health troubles :—liver troubles, nerves, dyspepsia, liability to stomach trouble and paralysis of the upper limbs. As a general rule the Mercurian is a healthy type, and frequently retains a youthful appearance in old age.

Upper Mars :—The Signs, either single or in combination, which add strength to this Mount, are the Triangle, Star, Circle, Single Vertical line, Trident, and Square. The Cross, Island, Cross-bars, Dot or Grille show defects of the Mount. All Cross-lines, Stars, Crosses or Grilles in the Plain of Mars increase inflammability and temper.

Signs on Lower Mars must be read on the Influence lines inside the Life Line.

Health troubles :—excitability, intestinal trouble, throat and bronchial troubles, and blood disorders. The Martians are as a rule robust and healthy.

Luna :—The Signs, either single or in combination, which

add strength to this Mount, are the Star, Trident, Circle, Square, Triangle, or Single Vertical lines. The Grille, Cross, Cross-bars, Islands, Dots, or badly formed Stars indicate defects.

Health troubles :—poor circulation of the blood, extreme nervousness, peritonitis, inflammation of the bowels, appendicitis, cholera, intestinal troubles, and cancer are shown on the Upper third of the Mount, The Lower third of the Mount shows kidney and bladder troubles. The Middle third of the Mount shows gout and rheumatism.

Venus :—The Signs, either single or in combination, which add strength to this Mount, are the Triangle, Circle, Square, or Single Vertical Line. The Cross, Grille, Island, or Dot indicate the defects.

Health troubles :—In low type Venusians we find venereal disease, shown by black dots or brown patches on the Mount or back of the hands. For other and general health troubles of the Type, the other Mounts, nails, and so on, must be examined.

PART TWO

CHEIROMANCY or PAST, PRESENT and FUTURE EVENTS as INDICATED by the LINES and MARKS on the HANDS

CHAPTER VI

THE CHARACTERISTICS OF LINES

WHEN examining the Lines of the Hand, the first important point to notice is the Character, i.e. their clearness, depth, evenness, whether they are perfect or defective, and if defective, the nature of the defect, how far it extends, and the condition of the Line following the defect.

The first general principal governing the Lines is that the more evenly they run, the clearer they are, the less they are crossed, broken, islanded or chained, and the nearer pink in colour, the better the line is, the more vigorous and clear will be the operation of its attributes. It must be remembered that vertical lines are favourable, while all horizontal lines crossing them are defects—this also applies to the Mounts.

Clear cut, even, pink lines are the best, for every obstruction or defect is inimical.

It must also be noted whether any one line is deeper or shallower than another, is more defective or differs in its character from the other lines in the hand. If the lines, in general, are of the same size and character, but one particular line is much deeper, clearer or better coloured, then the thing which this deep line indicates is the strongest.

If the lines are broad and shallow, they are weak ones, and will show weakness, vacillation and general discouragement. Lines that are deep, well cut in the hand, and well coloured, without being crossed or otherwise defective, show vigour and strength, steadiness of purpose, evenness of temper, and make for general success.

All the changes, obstructions and defects occurring to

FORKED LINES

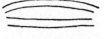

SISTER LINES

SPOTS ON LINE

ISLANDS

TASSELLED LINES

ASCENDING AND DESCENDING
BRANCHES

CHAINED LINES

BROKEN LINES

SQUARE ON LINE

+ X + X

CROSSES ON LINE

o U O

CIRCLES ON LINE

###

GRILLE ON LINE

△ ⩟ ◁

TRIANGLES ON LINE

THE FORK

✳

THE STAR

lines have special names, and these I will consider separately.

THE UNEVEN LINE :—This line may seem clear, but a close examination will show it to be deeper in some parts than in others. In parts, it will be thin, though at other times it may be broad and shallow—these alterations show changes in the character of the line—when deep, strong and vigorous ; when thin, vacillating and weak—thus we get unequal and spasmodic operation of the qualities of this uneven line.

The above indications are applicable to all the lines and not any particular line.

THE SPLIT LINE :—Fine lines branching from the main Lines or Split lines are often seen, and though at times they may run nearly parallel to the line from which they have split, they must not be mistaken for Sister Lines as these latter are entirely separate and distinct lines. Nor must they be accounted Islands, as they do not rejoin the line after splitting from it. In general, these Split lines show a weakening of the line during its continuance.

These Split lines are often the beginning of a new course in the life of a subject, in which case the Split line will grow in length. If the Split line only runs a short distance and then stops, it will show that an attempt to change the course of the life has failed. The wider these splits separate from the line, the more important they are, and the more likely to bring about a change in the course of the life. If a Split line runs to a Mount, it shows the attraction of the Mount, and the subject will either follow the qualities of the Mount or will seek the company of subjects of the Mount type.

The Split line will tell of many events, from a mere defect to a total change of life of the subject, and as such they merit close examination.

THE ISLAND :—This sign starts as a Split line, but after running a greater or less distance from the line from which it split, it turns back and rejoins its original line, thus forming a distinct loop to the line. Its size and length varies, but it is always a defect, and the extent of the island indicates the measure of its obstruction or duration, while from the point at which it is seen on the line, the age at which this weakening occurs can be read.

Breaks :—Are frequently seen, and always indicate a defect, but the kind of break will make a great difference as to its outcome. The wider the break the more serious it is. Broken lines may be repaired by the broken ends overlapping each other, or by a small cross line uniting them, by sister lines, or by a square enclosing the broken ends. Always a danger, they must be regarded seriously and from their size or the repair signs present, the outcome and effect must be estimated.

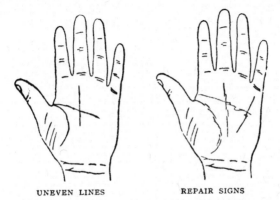

UNEVEN LINES   REPAIR SIGNS

One of the worst forms to be met is when the end of the line turns back after a break, especially if on the Life line; obviously this lessens the chance of repair, and it will generally result in disaster. Every turned-back line is a serious check, either to life, health, or career, according to the line on which it is found.

THE SQUARE :—Is an individual sign, and with but one exception always a good one. No matter what the breaks in a line or its menace, a Square around it will partially repair and minimise the danger. At times the Square is seen on a Mount, where it does not repair a break—such a Square indicates that the defects of the Mount will not predominate.

The exception to this general rule is a Square in the

upper portion of Mount Venus, near to the Life line ; in this position it indicates detention or incarceration.

THE FORK AND TASSEL :—These signs are found at the termination of lines. Some lines fade away until lost in the capillary lines of the skin ; some end abruptly, or with a cross or a dot, star or island, but often they terminate in a Fork or Tassel. These Tassels resemble a number of small short splits at the end of the line, and are often found at the end of a short Life line, Head or Heart line. But wherever found, they indicate the dissipation or gradual diffusion of the qualities of the line and the termination of its usefulness. If a Fork composed of two lines only terminates a line, it amounts to a split, and is not so bad as a Tassel.

THE DOT :—Is not so frequently seen, but is worthy of notice. It needs no explanation as to its appearance, but it varies in size and depth. Dots are always a defect, either on a line or as an independent sign. Small Dots are not serious and often appear after a bad illness, generally of a nervous character. They may be of any colour, and are always subject to repair by a good square.

THE CHAINED LINE :—This gives a line the appearance

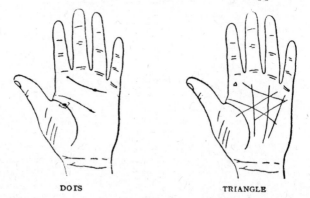

DOTS   TRIANGLE

of being made up of a number of small lines joined together, forming a line which is not clear, even or deep. This tells of a weak operation of the quality of the line it purports to be. If it is the Head line, it will show vacillation, want of self-control, headaches, and other brain disturbances. If only a portion of the line is thus chained, then the weakness only extends to the period covered by the defective line. The general mode of repair of such a defect is by a sister line or lines, running parallel to it.

THE TRIANGLE :—This is usually a single sign, though it is at times found on a line, and may be formed by the crossing of the main lines—but it is not then so strong as when seen as a single sign. When a well made Triangle is seen, not formed by the crossing of the main or minor lines, and the lines at the angles do not overlap, it tells of great Mental brilliancy of the Line, Mount or Finger on which it is found. It always refers to the Mental qualities only.

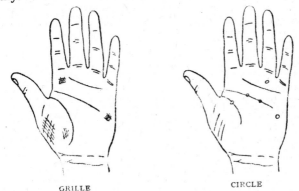

GRILLE   CIRCLE

THE GRILLE :—This sign is composed of a number of minute lines crossing each other at right angles or nearly so, and is always a serious menace. If very pronounced and composed of deep red lines, the danger is great ; if only made up of small thin lines, it is not so serious. On the Mounts it is a bad sign, bringing up its health defects or its bad qualities. A Grille composed of lines not running vertical and horizontal is not so serious a defect as one with the lines running more nearly at right angles.

CROSS-BARS :—These are constituted of horizontal lines lying close together, but without vertical lines crossing them. I have always found this sign to be worse than the Grille. This sign will bring out the worst side of a Mount, such as health defects, but fortunately it is not often seen. The deeper the lines composing it, the worse will be the indication.

THE CIRCLE is a very unusual sign, and is chiefly valuable when seen on the Life line or the Mount of Apollo—or the Line of Head under Apollo. Such a marking will tell of *delicacy* of the eyes. It is not found on the hands of *all* blind persons, but chiefly on the hands of those who have poor vision or weak eyes. It is said, by some Palmists, to have been seen on Mount Luna as a separate sign, and that it indicated death by drowning—but in all the years of my experience I have never seen it in this form.

THE TRIDENT, or three-pronged spear-head, is found at the upper end of the line. It is a favourable indication, and adds strength to the Line of Apollo, increasing its brilliancy and the chances of success. It is a very unusual marking and is always a good one. It must, however, be perfectly marked to ensure its fullest indication.

THE STAR is an important and valuable sign ; it is sometimes a good indication, but at other times a bad one according to its location. Whenever seen on the hand, it should be regarded as of the utmost importance. If small and evenly formed in all its proportions, it will mean brightness or intensification ; but if large, ill-formed and

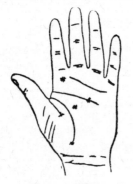

STAR   CROSS

diffused, it indicates a break-up or an abrupt ending.   On the Life line it will mean sudden death ; on the Head line mental trouble or insanity ; on a Voyage line death from drowning—wherever found, the large deep Star means danger.   On the Line of Apollo or Mount of Apollo, it will indicate unmeasured success—but the Star must be well formed and even.

THE CROSS is a very usual sign to be seen, though it appears sometimes as a single sign, or is formed by lines crossing other lines.   Always note the depth of the lines forming it and how they conform in proportion to the other lines.   A deep cut, highly coloured cross is of great import. The Cross is an obstacle or defect, and generally produces either a bad quality, a health defect, or a change in the course of the subject's life.   In any position it must be regarded as an unfavourable sign.

AGE ON THE LINES

When reading hands, I have always made a practice of asking the age of the subject, so as to enable me the more readily to distinguish the past from the present or future. The age given may not always be the correct one, but apart from a capability to read age from the physical indications, there is no other means of ascertaining the age of the subject.   The hand itself does not afford the necessary information ; nor is it possible (as frequently claimed) to come down to the month in which any event noted has happened or may happen ; the utmost that can be done is to fix the year, and to do that successfully requires a good deal of practice in reading age dates from the lines.

There are some Palmists who, in dealing with matrimonial questions, profess to be able to discern initials of names in the hands, others who can tell the subject's lucky day ; doubtless the same Palmists, if pressed, would venture to state what one would have for dinner on the morrow.   Anyhow they could do the one thing as easily as they could the other—but from the hand, it is utterly impossible.

In my method of reading the age of any past, present or future event, I have gone on the presumption that the average length of the life is seventy years, and I make my calculations as to date from the lines.   After many years of experience and daily practice, I can see no occasion for alteration—the diagrams herewith are sufficiently explicit and speak for themselves ; the principle is applicable to all hands, long or short.

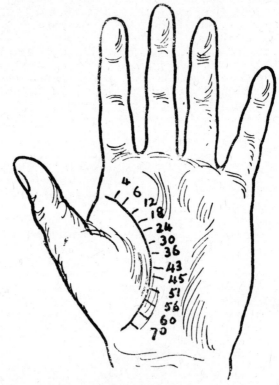

TIME ON THE LIFE LINE

It should be noted that on the Life Line Age is read downwards ; the Lines of Saturn, Apollo and Mercury are read upwards, while the Heart and Head Lines work from their starting point.   It is important to bear in mind that the Lines do not always run on the hands in the exact positions shown in the diagrams ; allowance must be made for variations, as no two hands are spaced alike, while a further difficulty for the beginner lies in the fact that one or more such lines may be absent.

To read the age correctly will require a lot of practice. As a rule beginners read age readily, but the experienced reader of hands is far more chary, and uses judgment in his fixings. The one and only essential to accuracy is practice, practice, and it requires a large amount of expertness to fix even *the year* when events shown will happen, or have happened.

CHAPTER VII

THE chief Lines of the Hand are shown and named in the accompanying illustration ; these are as recognised by all leading Palmists. But a brief investigation of hands will disclose the fact that, whilst it is possible to find hands with the lines fairly approximating to those in the diagram, yet by far the greatest number will show a great divergence in the position of the lines, while in a large number of cases, some of the lines will be entirely absent, others having one or more of the defects mentioned in Chap. IV.

As a matter of fact, no two hands are alike, not even one's own two hands. This may appear bewildering and nowhere is the old adage of "Many men many minds" more prominen ly manifest than in the lines or markings in the hands. Each and every variation has its distinct meaning, and it is for the Hand-reader to find it out, and apply its bearing on the Character, Health, Operations and Success of the subject.

To attempt to illustrate all the variations of the lines and their operations would be an impossible task ; the most that can be done is to illustrate how the varied conformations of the lines can be harmonised with the life and character of the subject, according to the generally accepted rules of the science. I shall treat each individual line in the order of its importance.

THE HEART LINE arises from some point under or near the finger of Jupiter, and then traces its course across the upper portion of the palm, under the Mounts, terminating on the percussion. It is of primary importance, as it deals with the mechanism which controls the life stream, and which so largely influences the health and temperament.

It is not often that this Line is entirely absent in the hand, but many hands will be seen with only one line crossing under the Mounts. It is not certain whether

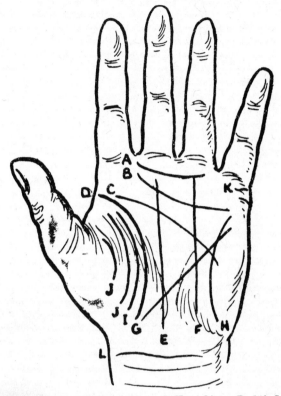

A. Girdle of Venus ; B. Heart Line ; C. Head Line ; D. Life Line ;
E. Line of Fate or Saturn ; F. Line of Success or Apollo ; G. Line
of Health or Mercury ; H. Line of Intuition ; I. Line of Mars ;
J.J. Influence Lines ; K. Lines of Affection ; L. Rascettes or
Bracelets.

such a line should be read as the Heart or the Head line,
or whether it should be treated as a joint line.   It is the
accepted practice, however, to assume that the Heart
line is absent, and that the single line seen is the Head
line.   The lines on the hand are controlled by the Brain,
and not by the Heart, and that is reckoned sufficient to
account for the Head line being present.

When the Heart line is absent, or doubled with the Head
line, it tells of a lack of sympathy and the affectionate side
of the disposition, and would indicate such a subject to be
selfish and cold-blooded, one who desires success even at
the expense and injury of others. It is a bad marking,

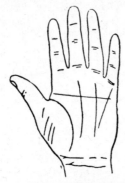

HEART LINE ABSENT
ALTOGETHER

HEART LINE MERGED
INTO HEAD LINE

for it readily leads from selfishness to hypocrisy, deceit,
want of candour, and even to dishonesty. If the Heart
line should be absent in both hands, it would tell of one
who lacks heart in a moral way ; a person who is cold,
selfish, cowardly, and sometimes a great bluffer or bully.

Hands are met which show the Heart line to be present
for a short distance, but then it turns down sharply and
becomes merged with the Head line. Such a marking
must not be mistaken for an absence of the Heart line ; a
close inspection of the hand, and particularly of the Head
and Life lines, will almost invariably show that the subject has been the victim of a heavy disappointment or loss,
which has resulted in a serious change in the temperament
and life. This sign, when seen, is at times marked in the
left hand only, the right hand possessing a regularly
marked and placed Heart line, indicating a return to
normal conditions. It is not often that such a marking
is seen, but I have often found it accompanied by a deflection of the Head line to the Plain of Mars in the right
hand, and at times in the Head line in both hands.

Usually this line has its starting point on or near the Mount of Jupiter ; sometimes it arises on Mount Saturn, and at times the line has forks or branches at its beginning, all of which may start from Mount Jupiter, or spreading out as a fan, extend as far as Mount Saturn.

There are, however, three well-verified readings attached to the three usual rising points of the Line. These are used as a basis, but subject to modification, and changed according to the variations in the starting point.

A. The Line rising from Mount Jupiter tells of the development of the *sentimental* side of the affections. The subject will be one to whom love is an ideal and an adoration—one, in fact, to whom love, even though accompanied with poverty, would prove an irresistible attraction.

B. When the Line rises between the Mounts of Jupiter and Saturn, it indicates the common sense and practical associated with the affections, and tells of one not carried away by sentiment ; one who would look on love in a cottage, without plenty to eat, as a delusion. There is nothing soft or sentimental about such a subject ; he or she is always sensible, not foolishly fond.

C. Rising from the Mount of Saturn, it tells of sensualism in the affections, a person whose love is more passionate than wise. This will certainly be the case if Mount Venus is large and pink or red in colour, with the lines of Life and Mercury strong. These indications will tell of physical desire (from the starting point of the Heart line) and of the necessary strength (as shown by the other lines) to carry out such desires.

When the Heart line arises from all three of these sources, it indicates the union of sentiment, common-sense and passion, and reveals the heart as the strongest factor in the subject. A strong, fine Head line and a good Thumb will be needed to prevent the Heart ruling the Head, as otherwise life must be more or less a failure. In this origin of the Heart line, note which of the three forks is deepest at its start, as this will be a guide as to which of the three will predominate.

The line sometimes starts with several forks on Mount

Jupiter ; in such a case the sentimentality of the subject is increased.

The general rule is that a single clear line makes the affections more self-contained. The deeper and clearer the line at its start, the deeper but more likely to be selfish are the affections. The more the line branches, the more the affections go out to others. The line starting with a fork tends to make the subject more successful in life by giving him many friends.

The Heart line inclining to the Head line at its start shews that the Head or reason is powerfully in the lead, and will be the deciding factor in matters in which the affections are concerned.

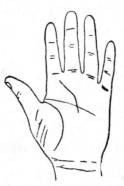

HEART LINE CUTTING THROUGH HEAD LINE

Should the Heart line start from the Head line, then your subject will be absolutely controlled as to his affections by the Head or reason, while if the Head line is deeper and clearer than the Heart line, it will be the more certainly so. When the Heart line, during its course, droops towards the Head line, then during the period that such deflection continues, the Head or reason will control.

In examining this line, its length must be considered, as it will tell of too much or too little heart. If the line, rising normally, runs but for a short distance and then stops, it will indicate that serious difficulty will beset the subject at the date at which it ends—although all the other lines of the hand may run on to their normal terminations. This sudden ending of the Heart line may mean either that the heart will cease to beat, or that the subject will possess but little feeling or affection for others. This sudden ending is a very poor indication.

Should the line entirely cross the hand from one side to the other, it tells of one who has too much heart, and who will in all things be guided only by sentiment ; he or she will be of a jealous disposition, and passionate in affection. The line must be examined in both hands, for if the above indications are seen only in the left hand, while the line in the right runs its normal course, then it will be found that a great improvement has been effected. But if the line is similar in both hands, then the conditions will be more certain.

The line of the Heart may at times be seen rising towards one of the Mounts, but rarely to more than one.

In such a case, it will indicate that the qualities of that Mount, or some person of the Mount type, will strongly attract the subject. But if the rise of the line merges into the particular Mount, and ends there, then the subject will have surrendered entirely to the attraction. It is not often that such an indication will be met, but slight deflections or risings will be seen, and should be noted. However great or small the deflection may be, it will tell of attraction sufficiently powerful to influence the life for the term of its duration.

The line deflecting towards the Head line will show that, at that time, the head and reason dominated sentiment, and that during the period it existed, there would be indifference to others, avarice and selfishness would be a marked characteristic. If the Heart line should, as a result, become merged in the Head line, cold reason will donimate the Heart. In such a case it will sometimes be seen, after a time, that the Heart line rises again towards its normal position. This indicates that the subject, later in life, regained some portion of the earlier disposition, but the effects of such a change cannot be entirely obliterated or overcome.

Should the Heart line deflect to such an extent as to cut *through* the Head line, instead of merging into it, or returning to its proper position, serious brain fever, the unbalancing of the mental faculties, or even death may result. In any event, the result is disaster—the Mount type of the subject will afford an indication as to the nature of the result. It is apt to occur at any point of the Heart line through the hand, and the age at which it occurs can be read from the line.

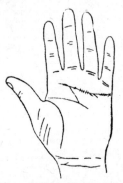

PHYSICAL DEFECTS ON HEART LINE

If a Star is seen at the point where the Heart line cuts the Head line in this way, the most serious consequences may be expected. An Island on the Head line after such a cutting will indicate that the result will be a delicate condition of the brain for the period covered by the Island. If the broken end of the Head line is cut by a bar, sudden death from heart failure may be looked for, and if such a bar is seen on *both* ends of the broken Head line, then death from heart disease will result. A Dot on both ends of the broken line will have the same result as a bar.

Breaks of all sorts and sizes are often met. In nearly every such case, one end of the broken line will go wide of its course, and thus afford a clue to the cause of the breach. They are always serious, even if small, and repair signs, if any, must be looked for. If the ends overlap each other, or have sister-lines joining them, or if a square surrounds them, read them as serious heart difficulties, prevented from a fatal end by such repair signs. When such Breaks are seen, examine the Life and Mercury lines for health difficulties, and if no such signs are seen, then read such Breaks as an interruption to the affections.

The termination of the Heart line is important. I have stated that it should run across the hand to the percussion in order to be normal, but it does not always do so—it

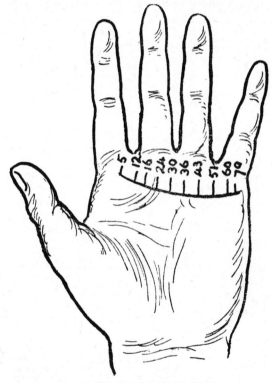

AGE SHOWN ON HEART LINE

may be seen starting under Jupiter and ending under Mount Saturn—such a line is not an indication of longevity. With this Heart line, the nails should be examined for indications of paralysis and heart disease ; also the Lines of Life and Mercury should be noted for defects as indicating illness, and if such are seen, then the life of your subject will probably terminate about the age of twenty-five years. Should, however, the subject be *above* that age, then the sign will indicate one who began life with warm affections, but changed entirely and became cold, selfish, distant and heartless at that age.

The line terminating on Mount Apollo tells of one who has surrendered to the ideal of Art and Beauty, or to some one of the Apollonian type—this, with the line rising on Mount Jupiter, will add ideal love to the Apollonian qualities. At the same time, with this ending, you should note the nails and the lines of Life and Mercury, for indications of heart disease or other defects of the Mount, to make sure that the particular termination is not a *health* defect.

The line terminating on Mount Mercury will tell of one largely affected by the finances ; money will influence love. It is not generally an indication of a health defect, but it is always advisable to note if there is any, as one never knows what may result.

The line terminating on Upper Mars will indicate that the Martian qualities attract, but as such a marking brings the Heart line in close proximity to the Head line, it will indicate a very secretive disposition.

If the Heart line should take a sudden sweep downwards to the Mount of Luna for its termination, the extra length of the Heart line will result in jealousy, increased by the force of imagination due to Mount Luna, which will make the subject most unhappy, as every trifle will be magnified into a tragedy.

It is not in itself a health defect, unless it crosses or cuts the Head line ; but if the line forms a curve and ends near the Life line on the Plain of Mars, the life will be endangered, and the subject will prove exceedingly irritable and changeable, excitable and difficult to get on with. With this Heart line, the Lines of Head, Life and Mercury must be examined as to its seriousness. Be especially careful with this marking not to confound it with the Line of Saturn—unless it rises well on Mount Jupiter, it must be read as the Line of Saturn, with the Heart line absent.

No two hands being marked alike, it would serve but

little purpose to overload the pages with diagrams ; nor is it possible to detail every variation of the line. The utmost I can do is to supply the general principle which governs it, and give an outline of the mode of reasoning out its varied combinations and changes.

The next important point in the Heart line to need consideration is the Character of the line, and in order to ascertain this, the line must be noted closely, not as a whole but sectionally. For the Heart line to be perfectly conditioned, it must be uniformly deeply cut and smooth, unmarred by breaks, islands or other defective markings, of proper length and well-coloured. The line then indicates strong affections and consistency in love matters; true, there may be but few love affairs, but when there are such, they will be strong and ardent but not over demonstrative. What is more to the purpose, the circulation will be good, and so will be the physical condition of the heart itself.

If the line is thin, there will be little care for others manifested ; the affections will be marked by selfishness, with no genuine affection for any one ; the subject will be narrow-minded, conventional and unsympathetic. The line, however, must be thin out of proportion to the other lines of the hand, and the type of the subject must be taken into account.

The next variation of the line is the Broad and Shallow ; this will disclose a measure of physical weakness of the heart, and as a necessary consequence the affections will correspond. There will be a good deal of fickleness in the affections, for such subjects easily fall in love and as easily fall out again. They are not always off with the old love before they are on with the new, for they are incapable of a deep and lasting affection. If all the lines in the subject's hands are of the same type, then be sure that in all things he is the same, vacillating and unreliable.

Next we have the Chained formation of the Heart line. With this formation, if the Mount of Venus is large, the subject is uncertain and variable in his affections—in a word a flirt. The heart's action, too, is irregular, its general condition is poor ; it indicates, especially if there is an Apollonian strain in the subject, a tendency to heart trouble, if not actual disease of the organ. For this the Life line must be noted at the same age, and if a Star is seen on the Life line at the age, the worst may be expected. You will also require to note whether the other lines are also chained ; if so, the defect is general.

Bear in mind that these thick, thin, broad and shallow, or chained qualities of the line only apply during the period they are seen on the line ; at any change in the character of the line, the subject will change. All such changes will result in a like change in the subject, and from these, the age at which they occur and their duration, they will form by themselves an interesting reading. But always remember that colour operates strongly on the Heart line, as well as any defects found on the line, as these latter have a direct bearing on either the affections or the health.

Split lines may either rise from the Mount or fall towards the Head line. The upward Split line usually rises to one or the other of the Mounts, and if not a health defect, it will tell of the influence of the Mount qualities attracting the subject, or that some person of the Mount type has proved interesting.

As a rule, the downward Split lines tell of a conflict between the Head and the Heart, and usually indicate disappointment or love sorrows.

Islands are always defects, and indicate a weak *physical* action of the heart. The size of the Island will show its seriousness.

Cross-bars cutting the line tell of constant heart irritations, either of illness, or more probably worries in the affections. If these Cross-bars cut the line in many places, it shows the trouble to be a continuous one during the period in which they appear.

Dots on this line I have found to be, as a rule, defects of the health, and their size will indicate their gravity. When I see them, I make it a practice to look closely for indications of heart disease, and of course the larger and deeper the Dot the more serious the trouble.

Stars on the Heart line will indicate illness or trouble in the affections. If illness, it will be heart disease, but if the Star is under Mount Saturn, rheumatism may be added. If the Star is large, well-formed, and its centre is on the Line, sudden heart failure is indicated at the age on which the Star is seen on the line.

NORMAL POSITION OF HEAD LINE

THE HEAD LINE

The importance of this line cannot be over-estimated, seeing that it indicates the nature of the mental qualities, and tells of the character of the mind, which operates through the brain and manifests itself on this line. Hence it is rarely absent from the hand, though other lines may be missing.

The commencing point of this line will most often be found to be from the Life line, to which it is slightly attached, before it branches away across the Plain of Mars. At times it may be found starting at various points lower down the Life line, but the sooner the line separates from the Life line the sooner the subject will begin to think for himself or herself. Starting lower down the Life line, less self-confidence will be manifest, the more dependent will the subject be upon others, and the later in life will the subject begin to exercise self-reliance.

Its course should be in a somewhat sloping direction, towards the percussion, either falling to Mount Luna, sometimes rising to Mount Mercury, or running in a more or less straight line across the hand. This *straight* Head line. in the absence of the Heart line, is not a nice line, though it brings success of a kind, by reason of its disregard for others, for it can be avaricious, cold, heartless, and extortionate. The colour test should be applied to it, as for the hands themselves. It tells by its length of abundant mentality.

If, on the other hand, the Head line is short, it will indicate that the subject is not mentally strong; while if the Life line is short, it may mean that the life will be short—certainly so if the short Head and Life lines end with a Star. If seen only in one hand, then such will be threatened, hence both hands must be closely considered on this line, and in fact when dealing with all the lines.

In every case the Head line should be of a good length, even in depth and clearness, not broken or otherwise defec-

HEAD LINE WIDELY SEPARATED
FROM LIFE LINE SHOWING
RECKLESSNESS

HEAD LINE RISING
FROM JUPITER

tive—then the judgment will be good, the head sound, the sense strong, with good intellectual faculties. A broken, defective, descending, or pale line indicates weakness, headaches, want of fixity of ideas, and irresolution.

When the line commences quite apart from the Life line, the subject will not be deficient in self-confidence, and may even possess a measure of conceit. This formation is often successful, owing to the belief in oneself which is developed, enabling the subject to smile at criticism. Should the line be widely separated from the Life line, there is a strong tendency to recklessness and carelessness ; while if the Mount of Mars is well developed and clear, and the Head line also long, deep and clear, it will result in bravery, amounting to rashness and foolhardiness.

If this widely separated line is short and weak, there will be jealousy as well as carelessness.

The line rising from Mount Jupiter will show a person ambitious, with good capability for leadership, self-confident, reliant. With a strong clear line, it is always an indication of keen mentality ; the subject is diplomatic and brainy, and, other things being equal, he will be successful in his life's pursuits.

The line may at times be seen rising inside the Life line, on the Lower Mount of Mars, and after crossing the Life line, it continues towards the Percussion. This will indicate a person who is vacillating, one who will start many things with great enthusiasm, but gradually drop them. The subject will prove a 'shifter,' rarely successful, always aggressive, and frequently in trouble.

At times, with the line rising from the Life line, a branch line from it is seen rising to Mount Jupiter. This will show that strong ambition will rule the possessor. If the hand in such a case is purely mental, then mental fame will be the ambition. If artistic, then fame will be sought in Art ; but if the hand is material, then the attainment of wealth will be the dominant aim.

In all readings of the Head line, the significance of the finger tips, and the Three Worlds of Palmistry, must be brought to bear on the subject, as indicating the natural trend of the mental qualities—nor must the character of the Thumb be overlooked.

Having considered the various points from which the line may be found to arise, the *course* of the line next demands attention. The more direct, strong and clear the line runs, and the less it is changed in its course, the more fixed are the ideas, the more even the mental balance, and the more practical and commonsense are the views.

Normally the line curves slightly upwards at its start,

and generally this curve is about midway between the Mounts of Jupiter and Saturn. When the line perceptibly curves beneath Mount Saturn so that its course is changed, it will show that the subject is strongly tinged with Saturnian ideas—thus, in all cases of similar curvings of the line to other Mounts, the qualities of such Mounts will be applicable to them.

The line is subject to variations throughout its whole length, and when such occur, both hands must be noted, for if the variations are only in the left hand, whilst they are absent from the line in the right, it will indicate that the quality or character of the line has improved, or vice versa.

Amongst such variations will be found :—

The Wavy or Undulating Line : this may exist for only a portion of its length or throughout the line. This condition will tell of want of fixity of ideas, during such period as it exists on the line, combined with vacillation, changeableness, and want of self-reliance at that age, and during the length of time for which it endures. The cause of this condition may be found on the Life or Mercury lines.

Deflections of the line. At times the line will be seen deflected downwards, at others upwards, while instances of both may be seen on the same line. The straight form but slightly drooping line, marks the normal condition. Generally speaking, all rising deflections are uplifting in their effects, while all downward variations indicate a period of depression, or a dispirited and unsatisfactory condition. If the deflection is short, the subject soon returns to practical ideas. With all deflections, up or down, observe the character of the line both before, during, and after the deflection, as this will show the result. If before the deflection, the line is deep, clear and well-cut, while it is seen thin during the change and is chained after, it will show that before the alteration the mind was strong and vigorous, during the deflection it became less vigorous, while it was impaired afterwards, at ages to be read on the line.

If the line is thin at its start, chained during the deflection, and terminates in a Star, it will tell of one who starts with a weak mind, which was impaired by whatever caused the deflection, and ends in a break-up, indicating either insanity or death—to ascertain which look to the Life line, nails, type, etc.

When the Head line rises and merges itself into the Heart line, it will show that sentiment has overcome reason. It may, in weak cases, indicate criminality, as the subject will lose self-control, and may be led to commit crimes in response to a direct appeal to the passions. If the hand is coarse in type, Mount Venus large, full and red, the Heart line deep and red, the nails short, and

HEAD LINE CURVED
UNDER SATURN

HEAD LINE MERGING
INTO HEART LINE

Mount Mars large, you will have a subject who would become criminal in order to gratify his or her desires.

In many hands, you will see the line sloping more or less towards Mount Luna; this shows that the subject is somewhat influenced by the imagination, and is not practical to the exclusion of all else. If the line is good, deep, well-cut, and clear of defects, the slope is immaterial; in fact, it is essential for authors, speakers, linguists, and successful professional men. But with this indication, as with all others, excess may make it bad. It is only when the sloping line is seen on a poor type of subject, or when it is thin or defective, that it is unfavourable.

The line sloping low down on Mount Luna, and terminating with a Star, indicates insanity—should the line terminate by being chained, instead of a Star, it will indicate a check to the mentality, and mental impairment; a Cross terminating the line will have the same effect, but should this line end in an Island, Dot or Break, the result will be mental disturbance.

If the Head line ends in a slight fork, it shows versatility, and if the fork is a strong and wide one, the subject will possess strong practical views as well as imagination. In a good hand, this is a fine marking, but it often leads to irregularity; for instance, in a bad hand, this marking will indicate the liar.

At times the Head line may be divided into three well-cut forks, one going towards Mount Mercury, one towards Mount Mars, and one towards Mount Luna. This is a splendid marking, showing great diversity of intellect, adaptability and versatility; it unites the business qualities of Mount Mercury, the resisting power of Upper Mars, with the imagination of Mount Luna, and invariably brings success, unless indolence, lack of ambition, or some other defect is strongly marked.

It is important to note the Character of the line, as this will disclose the strength or weakness of the mental qualities, as well as the capability for concentration or otherwise.

The deep and well-cut line shows good mental power, self-control, fixity of purpose, and the possession of a good memory; it will indicate one who does not lose his head in a critical time, but is even-tempered, well-balanced and capable of carrying out his plans. If the Head line is long, deep and well-cut, its length will show great mental power, and its depth strength of this quality. Long Head lines are often seen to be broken or otherwise defective; the subjects may be very bright, but the line has no steadiness and is unstable in its action. A strong Thumb added to a deep, well-cut Head line will make the subject firm, cool and irresistible.

If the hand and lines in general are small, and the Head line only is deep and well-cut, it is dangerous, as it indicates that the mental power is too strong for the physical strength to carry.

Many hands are to be seen in which the Head line is thin

and narrow, and traces itself but lightly across the hand; such a line shows mental delicacy—the subject may be clever, and will be so, if the line is long, but a want of mental vigour will be manifest. With these thin lines on the hands of those who make great mental exertions, there may often be seen places where the line is deeper— such deeper place will indicate the periods when the mental pressure has been too great, and if continued may lead to nervous prostration or paralysis. Subjects with thin Head lines should never risk burning the candle at both ends; the mental strength should be conserved.

VACILLATION

STAR ON HEAVILY SLOPING
HEAD LINE, SHOWING
INSANITY

Stars, Crosses or Dots on the Thin line show danger to the mental life which must not go unheeded. Cuts or small lines crossing the Head line, if frequent, will indicate headaches, and if deep on a thin line will indicate brain fever, nervous breakdown, or even paralysis.

In all examinations, note both hands, for if the lines are deep in the left hand and thin in the right, the strong brain power shown by the deep line has been weakened. Should the line in the left hand be thin and the line in the right hand deep, then the brain power has been increased. The same examination should be made with respect to all the lines and the same reasoning applied—unless the subject is naturally left-handed; in such case the left hand being the operative one must be accounted as the right hand.

The Broad and Shallow Line shows one who is not resolute, firm and courageous, but who is undetermined, vacillating, uncertain, wanting in self-reliance and with poor self-control, little concentration and a poor memory—but, as in the case of the deep and thin lines, both hands must be examined.

The main *defects* to be seen on the Head line are uneven lines, Splits, Cross-bars, Islands, Dots and Breaks, and chained lines.

The Chained Line is a bad indication, and tells of one weak, vacillating, timid, sensitive and changeable—the memory is poor, judgment bad, and headaches will be frequent ; the ideas are impractical and in speculative matters not to be trusted. If the line is only partially chained, the above condition will apply to the period of the chaining only, but both hands must be examined.

The Uneven Line is one in which the thick and thin appearance alternates during its whole course or a portion of its course ; these alterations show changes in the mentality from strength to weakness. If a Star, Dot or Cross occurs in the course of this Uneven line, there is a risk of paralysis, apoplexy or insanity. The greatest care is needed by its possessor, who should avoid excitement, indulge in plenty of sleep, and whenever this line is seen the subject should be so advised.

SPLITS are frequently seen on the Head line. As a general rule, all rising Splits are better than those which fall from it. If the rising Splits are small and frequent, they will tell of mental aspirations and a desire to rise in position. If they are large and long, the head will be influenced by too many things and vacillation will result. If the Splits are downwards from the line, they will tell of discouragements and a want of mental vigour.

The Split often shows the pulling force of some attraction, the nature of which can be gathered from the place to which it extends. If a Split line runs to the Mount of Apollo, then the attributes of that Mount attract, and if it ends in a Star there will be success ; but should a Dot, Cross or Island end the Split, there will be failure. A

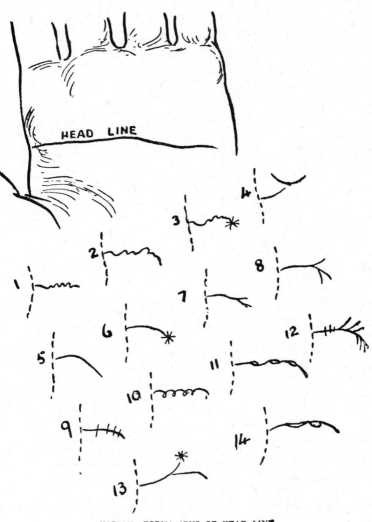

HEAD LINE

VARIOUS FORMATIONS OF HEAD LINE

similar reading applies to Splits rising to the other Mounts. Split lines rising and touching the Heart line show that sentiment, love and affection, occupy the thoughts, and if such a line merges into the Heart line, then sentiment will be the ruling power.

ISLANDS when seen on the line indicate that at the time of their occurrence the mental force is lessened. They always show a defect in the Constitution during their presence, and if the subject is put to any undue excitement or mental strain during the period covered by the Island, the mind may become unbalanced.

In hands covered by fine lines crossing in all directions, it will be safe to read the Islands as periods of mental unbalance. The subject whose hands are free of these fine Lines will be of phlegmatic temperament and without nervous strain ; he may avoid the danger incident to the Islands by his naturally calm and even temper. The Island, however, is a grave danger in every case, where seen on the Head line. The Character of the line before and after the Island must be noted in order to estimate the result fully and properly. Carefully look for any Chance (fine) lines which may have run from the Island to any other part of the hand, as these will often show that diseases peculiar to the Mount type of the subject have caused the Islands.

DOTS in the line are acute disorder, more or less severe according to the size and colour of the Dot. If small and white or pink, the trouble is an illness but not of a grave nature. If large and deep, red or purple in colour, then the brain trouble is severe and great care will be required at the age at which it occurs. The Character of the line following the dot will indicate the result.

BREAKS in the line produce irregular action, lack of concentration, want of firmness and self-control. They may be illnesses, in which case they will be corroborated from the nails, Life line, and other indications of disease. They often are to be seen on the hands of flighty, nervous and changeable subjects, but there is illness present each time the line breaks—the age at which this occurs can be seen from the line.

With every such break, look for repair signs, such as

sister lines, the overlapping of the ends of the broken line, connecting bars or squares. Should, however, the end of the broken line turn towards any Mount, then read it as in the case of a split line running to a Mount. Wherever the broken end goes, it will show the force which produced the break—be sure to notice the character of the line after the break.

STARS on the line are always a danger, and often indicate an operation, the nature of which will be found in other parts of the hand. In many cases a chance line from the Star will run to some indication as to the nature of the trouble. Crosses also are dangerous, and if large and deep may be counted nearly as serious as a Star.

The Head line is undoubtedly a very important line and constitutes the window of the mind, but in the reading of it the character of the Thumb must be taken into account.

It is absolutely essential to examine both hands, as the line will be found to be vastly different in many hands, and for every such divergence there is a reason. I have seen in the left hand of a subject the Head line drooping very low on Mount Luna, showing that imagination, the love of romance, and hopefulness were strong. In the right hand the Head line showed with a deflection downwards from twenty-five years of age to thirty-five, and then the line went straight across the palm to the percussion. I noted the hand as a whole, and told the subject that in his earlier years the writing of romance had been his hobby, but that at about the age of twenty-five friends had interfered, and that the bitter disappointment had completely changed the mental aspirations and destroyed the imagination ; the mind, now void of romance, was if anything too practical—the reading was admitted to be accurate.

Much the same may be seen as regards the commencement of the Head line. In the left hand I have seen it well separated from the Life line, while in the right it did not leave the Life line until about thirty years of age— the health was good, but in the palms of the hands, at about the age of twenty-three, there was a distinct hollow. There was also a line from Mount Luna crossing the Life line at the same age.   It then became apparent to me that the change in the commencement of the Head line had resulted from a disappointment in love ; the reading was confirmed on the Life and Heart lines, and was admitted to be accurate.

I mention these two examples to emphasize the necessity of reading both Head lines ; where there is any

WAVY HEAD LINE, SHOWING WANT OF FIXITY OF IDEAS

doubt as to the cause of changes, bring into requisition the whole hand—type, colour, nails—in fact, everything to ensure accuracy.

THE LIFE LINE

This line rises at the side of the hand, well under the finger of Jupiter ; encircling the Mounts of Lower Mars and Venus, it terminates in most cases under Mount Venus.   The line should be well cut, clear of defects, not broad and shallow, and continuous ; not too red in colour, nor too pale, but rather pink.   The colour tests are peculiarly applicable to it.

The line indicates the health of the subject during the various periods of life, and also whether the course of the life is upwards or downwards, and in many instances it shows the probable termination of life.

This line is rarely absent ; indeed, its total absence

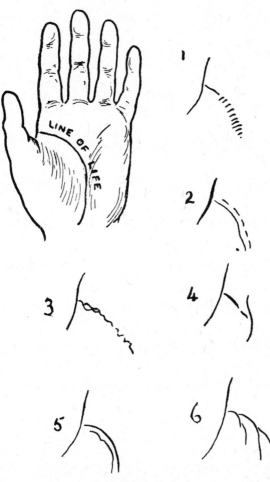

VARIOUS FORMATIONS OF LIFE LINE

would show that the life of the subject was extremely precarious, and that death might come at any moment. At this stage let me say that a strong Thumb and a good Head line will often carry the poorest Life line beyond its natural ending ; it is never possible to say that life will end at a certain age, for a strong will or vigorous brain can often wrest life from death.

There will arise in some hands a difficulty in distinguishing the Life line from the Line of Saturn (Fate line), or from the Line of Mars ; or even from the Strong Influence lines which are found inside the Life line. As a general guide, the Life line should enclose Mount Venus, and not run on top of it.

The Line usually rises at the side of the hand *under* Mount Jupiter, for this is its normal source and marks the start of the life. At times, however, it may be seen to rise upon Mount Jupiter ; this will indicate that the life will be a most ambitious one, filled with desire for success, wealth or fame, and that the subject will take every opportunity to form the acquaintance of people of note. Beyond this variation, it is very seldom that the Life line rises from any other source. The line varies but little in its course through the hand—the chief change is when the line runs closer to the Thumb, thus reducing the size of Mount Venus and making the subject cold and unsympathetic. This also diminishes the length of the life. It may in other hands be seen sweeping wide out into the palm of the hand, increasing the force of Mount Venus, and making the subject ardent, warm, generous and sympathetic. This of course lengthens the line, and adds strong vitality to the constitution. This is shown in the illustration of the Life line.

As a general proposition, the longer the Life line, the longer will be the life, and the shorter the line the shorter the life. Experience, however, shows that this general proposition is capable of much variation. The fact is the Life line shows the *natural* vigour and health of the subject. It must be remembered that death is not shown alone on the Life line—the lines of the Head, Heart and Mercury also show death indications, while it is indicated by Chance lines and individual signs as well. Hence in all cases of importance, it is absolutely necessary to compare the line in both hands.

In my many years of experience as a professional Palmist, I have found that a careful consideration of the

Life line alone, will enable me to give a good general and accurate summary of the life of a subject. From its varied characteristics the line will tell of many incidents regarding the affections, periods of dissatisfaction and gloom, as well as hope, success and health, and from the Chance lines running from it the causes thereof. It is used also, by many Palmists, as the one line from which to calculate ages ; but this is incorrect, as the age at the happening of events can just as easily be read on the other lines.

There is, however, one age which neither the hands nor the lines can supply—the age of the subject. This must either be obtained direct from the subject, or guessed.

In order to appreciate fully the value of the Life line, it is essential that the *Character* of the line should be studied closely—if the line is deep and well-cut and free from defects, the subject will be strong, vigorous and full of vitality, will resist disease and have few illnesses.

The deepest lines are seen in the hands of those having the least sensitive nerves, and consequently the fewest lines. If the line is long, as well as deep-cut and clear, the vitality and robustness will continue during the entire life. Unfortunately there are few such to be seen, as the majority of Life lines grow thin towards the end, thus marking the natural fading of the life force.

A Narrow and Thin Line will tell of less vitality, less resistive power against illness, and a greater liability to go under in health troubles. Should this line be thin, while all the other lines in the hand are deep and well-cut, the subject will be continually over-strained to the detriment of the health.

A line that is broad and shallow tells of an utter lack of vitality ; those possessed of such a line become very easy victims to all sorts of health troubles ; their constitutions are weak, and there is an absence of energy and push. Such a line on a soft and flabby hand evidences the extreme of laziness. With this line, examine the Mount of Saturn carefully ; if it is large or defective, the subject will be melancholy, gloomy and wretched. It is a most undesirable line to have.

A line running like a Ladder (page 108) has the same general effect as a Broad and Shallow line. The health will be very unreliable, and the subject is not only delicate, but there will be frequent illnesses, all more than ordinarily severe. See also Fig. 1 among "Various Formations of Life Line."

Sometimes the line will be composed of several fine lines, instead of being a single deep line. The subject will have an intensely nervous condition of health, and will be subject to great delicacy, and liable to suffer from general debility. See Fig. 2.

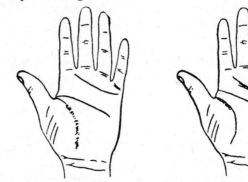

LADDERED LIFE LINE   CHAINED LIFE LINE

A Chained condition of the line always indicates delicacy and repeated suffering from annoying illnesses. If chained throughout the whole length of the line, ill-health will always be present ; but if only covering a portion of the line, the delicacy will extend during the continuance of the chain.

Sometimes you may see the course of the line interrupted—it is in part an unsatisfactory marking, and tells of delicacy in childhood, up to about the age of twelve years, when the health improves, though the subject is far from strong and robust. At about the age of thirty years, another period of great delicacy would be experienced, lasting about three years. On the recovery from this, the health would be restored, and the subject would become more robust and vigorous. As a matter of fact there are periods in almost everyone's life when he is stronger than at others. Even a weak constitution will have periods of better health from time to time, and such periods will generally be indicated by an uneven Line of Life.   See Fig. 3.

All lines which cut the Life line produce a defect.   In some cases, especially with very nervous persons, the Line is often crossed by a number of minute fine lines which do not actually *cut* the line.   These fine lines show a person who worries as the result of an intensely nervous condition ;   such a subject is very liable to small illnesses.

If there are fine Cross-bars on the line, they will show as many illnesses of a minor nature as there are Cross-bars.   On the other hand, if the Cross-bars are deep, and actually cut the line, they will indicate severe illness. The age can be determined from the line.

If a Cross-bar cuts through the Life line and terminates on Mount Saturn in a Grille, the illness will be a defect on Mount Saturn.   Should it end at a Dot, Island or break in the Heart line under Mount of Apollo, the illness will be heart disease, and the result will be shown by the Heart line, or by the termination of the Life line.

A Cross-bar running to a Wavy line of Mercury will indicate either jaundice or severe bilious fever.   The Cross-bar terminating in a Grille on Upper Mount Mars shows the illness to be either some blood disorder, or throat or bronchial troubles ;   if the latter the nails will confirm it.   If the Cross-bar terminates in a Grille or Cross, on Upper Mount Luna, then bowel trouble or intestinal inflammation will be indicated.   When the Cross-bar runs to Middle Mount Luna, and terminates there with the Mount grilled, gout or rheumatism is the trouble. This will be the more certain if a line with an Island on it runs to Mount Saturn—this latter indication is thoroughly reliable, even though there is no Grille or Cross on Mount Luna.   The Cross-bar going to a Grille or Cross on the Lower Mount of Luna will indicate the trouble to be with the kidneys or bladder, or female disease.   Running to a Ladder-like line of Mercury, it shows that the illness will come from the stomach, while if it should run to an Islanded line of Mercury, throat and lung trouble will cause the illness.

After any defect of the Life line, note carefully the

effect on the line itself. Often it will be found that the Cross-bars cutting the Life line begin on Influence lines on Mount Venus, in such cases you may safely conclude that worry concerning an Influence brought on the trouble.

ISLANDS on the Life line always indicate a period of delicacy, and the point where the Island begins marks the commencement of the delicacy, which will continue until the Island ends, provided that the line is good later on. If the line contains a series of Islands, then its operation will be that of a chained line and its effects will be the same.

ISLANDS ON LIFE LINE   BREAKS IN LIFE LINE

Whenever an Island is seen on the line, a close search of the hand should be made for health defects on the Mounts and lines, in order to discover the cause of the Island, if no cross-bars or fine lines run from the Life line to the defect.

It is very common to see an Island in the Life line in a woman's hand, at ages varying from forty to about fifty, as this is the usual period of the change of life, and the length of the Island will tell its duration. If with such an Island there is a Grille on Lower Mount Luna, female weakness will add its trouble to the change, and the character of the line after this Island will show the result.

DOTS are not often seen on the line, but they indicate

acute illness or accidents, and if the latter, there is often a Star under or in the vicinity of the Head line.   The Dots vary in size from a barely noticeable pin-point to a hole large enough to destroy the line.   They are of all colours, and they must be estimated in their effects by their size and colour.

White Dots are practically harmless ; Red Dots indicate febrile tendencies, while the deeper the dot and colour the more certain the reading.   They are, in all cases, useful as a means of locating a period of special import in the life of the subject, and will as a rule precede Islands, Chains, and other defects, thereby showing the severity of the illness.   A Dot on the line, followed by an Island and a chained line, and having a fine Chance line running to a Dot, small Island, Cross or Star on the Head line, will tell you of an attack of brain fever which undermined the health.   If a Dot on the line is connected by a fine line to a Cross on the Mount of Saturn, it will indicate an accident.

BREAKS in the line are often seen, and vary in their seriousness according to the character of the line, the width of the break, and how it is repaired.   Thus a break in a deep strong line would be far less serious than one occurring in a broad and shallow or a chained one.

All breaks in the line are important, as they indicate changes in the aspect of the life, as well as being checks or impediments to the health—as a rule from illness or accident.   The character of the line before and after the break must be considered, for if in the earlier years the line runs close to the Thumb and then a distinct break is seen when the line widens out, deep and well-cut, into the hand, it will show that at the age of the break or change in the line, the life (which hitherto had been monotonous and devoid of natural enjoyment) suddenly expanded and became fuller and happier.   In such a case, the fine line connecting the two portions of the line removes the change from the category of an actual break.   At times this may be seen the other way about, and the changed line will run closer to the Thumb ; a change for the worse is then indicated.   See Fig. 4.

I know as a fact from long experience and observation that any deflection of the line towards the Thumb lessens the pleasantness of the life by restricting the operation of the Mount of Venus. Naturally all deflections outwards *into the palm* increase the powers of the Mount, in each case during the years covered by the deflection.

It is difficult to solve the question whether a break indicates an accident ; but if the health in other ways is good, it should be taken as indicating an accident, as ill-health would be shown by other signs.

Small breaks which are at once repaired are not any more serious than dots or islands ; but wide breaks unrepaired are serious and a menace to life.

When the broken ends of the Life line turn back like a hook, the danger is grave, and the wider the break and stronger the hook the more hopeless will be the condition. In every case, the character of the line before and after the break must be noted carefully to determine the extent and nature of the injury or otherwise. Breaks may be repaired by the ends of the lines overlapping each other, by a sister line running close to the line where broken, by a square enclosing the break, and in other ways.

SPLITS are often seen and tend to reduce the strength of the constitution. Sometimes they are fine and hair-like, when they are harmless, and if they are rising upwards, they will show an upward trend of the life. But if they turn downwards, then their starting point will indicate the turning point of the life downwards. The rising lines sometimes run to one or other of the Mounts, which indicates that the quality of the particular Mount will influence the life from the starting point of the Split line.

These Split lines vary in strength ; if they are long and strong, they will tell of new ventures being undertaken, at times leading to a complete change in the life—in such cases, the Lines of Saturn and Apollo will indicate the result.

At times a break—connected with the original Life line by a small line—will be met, and the Life line from such break will run wide out in the Palm, ending near the rascette. This indicates as a rule a long residence over the seas ; often in these cases a strong Split line may be seen running to Mount Saturn, showing that such voyage resulted in a change in the career ; the result will be seen on the Lines of Saturn and Apollo.

The termination of the line varies in different hands, and can be seen at varying periods. A line that is long, strong and deep-cut may end equally strong ; it simply ends. In such a case, the subject will be strong to the end, with no lingering illness or wasting disease ; the Head and Heart lines and the type of the subject will disclose the cause of the ending.

When a line begins deep and strong, but gradually becomes thinner as it traces its course through the hand,

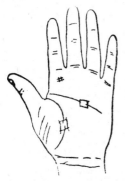

THE SQUARE—A REPAIR
SIGN ON LIFE LINE

SPLIT LIFE LINE, SHOWING
VOYAGE AND CHANGE OF CAREER

until it fades and disappears, it will tell of the gradual decrease of the vitality, until death from exhaustion ensues. A good Head line and a strong Thumb are of great value with such a line.

Forks at the end of the Life line show a waning of the vitality, and they weaken the Line ; but if the Forked line lies close to the Life line, its effect on the health is less marked than a widely forked end. When the line ends in a triple fork, then the dissipation of vitality is the more complete.

A Tassel at the end of the line shows the entire loss of vitality and consequent death. A Cross at the termination of the line foretells death at the age at which it is seen, and a similar result follows when the Line terminates with a Dot, Cross-bar or Star. But before coming to a final decision, carefully compare the line in both hands.

Crosses will, at times, be seen at various points of the Life line; the Lines of Saturn and Apollo may furnish indications of some change in the career, occasioned by sickness or accident. Stars on the Life line are always a menace to the life, and as a rule mean sudden death at the age indicated by their appearance, or some unusually severe shock to the system.

At times there will be seen a sort of double Life line, either running throughout the whole length of the line,

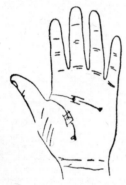

FORK AND TASSEL ON LIFE LINE   SPLIT LIFE LINE

or for a part of it only. This second line will lie close to the Life line, and is termed a Sister line. When seen, it has the effect of increasing the vitality and power of endurance during its continuance, as well as being a protection against any defects shown in the Life line. See Fig. 5.

It is not unusual to find the Life line having (apparently) two starting places—the later one starting from the Head line. This will tell that your subject was hindered in the early course of the life, the real life commencing at the later date. I have seen this change marked as low as thirty years. The reason for this may often be found in the home surroundings, circumstances presenting for a time insuperable difficulties to the start. See Fig. 6.

As the Life line varies in the two hands, I strongly emphasize the necessity of comparing the Line in each hand, remembering that a weak line in the left hand may be remedied by a strong one in the right—where defects are seen only in the left hand, they will be possibilities, which may not occur.

Although the line *apparently* shows the termination of life, it is exceedingly unwise to attempt to foretell the date of death as shown on the line—a good Head line and strong Thumb can accomplish much in postponing the stroke of doom.

It is always wiser to assume that the Life line shows the inherited physical constitution ; its termination on the hand indicates, therefore, the length of life, say, from the point of view of an Insurance Company. But illness or accident may shorten the life, just as vitality and mental vigour can and does lengthen it.

THE LINE OF SATURN

COMMONLY KNOWN AS THE FATE LINE

This line indicates the natural kind of career of the subject, and whether it will be successful, settled, or varying and changeable. It is not often absent, but when this happens, it does not indicate a purely negative existence. In the course of my career, I have met several successful business men in whose hands the line was absent ; I found them glorying in the fact that they were "self-made men," and by their own energy they had surmounted the handicap of the absent line.

There is no regular starting point for this line—it starts from many places, and not always even at the base of the hand. But start where it may, it always runs towards the Mount of Saturn. It will sometimes be found rising from the *inside* of the Life line ; then, if it runs on to the Mount of Saturn, it will tell not only of material success in life, but that near relatives will afford assistance. If it takes its rise from Mount Luna, and runs to the Mount of Saturn, then success will be attained, but one of the opposite sex will largely assist—this aid may be given either by advice and suggestion, or money. Rising from the centre of the palm and running to its Mount, the subject will attain success chiefly by his own efforts, and will be, in fact, the architect of his own fortunes.

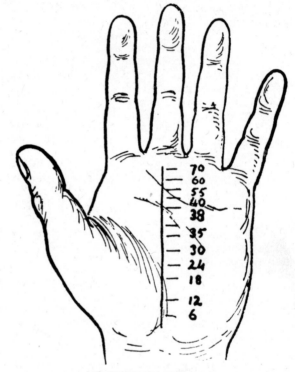

AGE SHOWN ON FATE LINE

When the line rises higher up in the hand, it will indicate that the subject will lead a more or less negative early life, and that it will not be until the line starts that the best period of his life will begin. The higher in the hand the Line starts, the later in life will the best period commence—the explanation will be found in some defect in one or more of the other lines or else on the Mounts. If it is seen that the line rises low in the left hand, but starts higher in the right, then you may be sure that something in the way of health, laziness, or the influence of family—possibly a disappointment in love—has caused the alteration in the original plan of the life.

This line is subject to variations as to its *Character*, for unless it is as deep as the other lines in the hand, the indications of the line will be out of their proper proportions, and it will not operate so well as if it balanced with the other lines. If it is very deep and well-cut, the subject will possess good capabilities, the right use of which will undoubtedly bring success. If this deep line extends to the Mount, then the favourable conditions will continue during the life.

If the line, however, should be short, the good conditions will be present only during the length of the line— the age can be read from the line itself. The line being *Thin* will show that though there are natural advantages present, great exertion will be needed for their full development.

A *Broad and Shallow* line is little better than having no line ; while if this line is the only one of this character, while the other lines are well and clearly marked, life will be one continual struggle.

The *Chained* line will make the career a hard one, but if the chaining is only of a part of the line, the difficulties will be confined to the period in which the chaining is seen. This reading of the characteristics will apply during any part of the line in which they are seen, and its alterations will show the "ups and downs" of life which come to most of us.

All defects, whether in the character of the line, or indicated by the following individual signs, are important, as they show how many impediments will occur, and how serious they will prove, while the condition of the line afterwards will tell their effect. All defects in the beginning (at the base of the hand, for this is the first of the lines to be read from the rascette upwards) refer to the childhood and usually are due to ill-health, the influence of parents, and the surrounding conditions—as the line grows deeper and better-cut, you will read it as difficulties overcome.

The line is also subject to defects occasioned by the presence of what are known as Individual signs. Islands on the line at times indicate conjugal infidelity, or in a woman's hand and with a chance line running from Luna to it, love for a married man, or moral depravity affecting the tenor of the life. Often they indicate financial difficulties or troubles, which continue during the existence of the Island. An Island, if seen at the start of the life, obviously could not be read as personal conjugal infidelity; some such trouble concerning one of the parents might affect the home life of the subject, or it might be caused by the financial difficulties of the parents, or by prolonged delicacy of health.

Cross-bars cutting the line are impediments to the career; each bar is a separate impediment, and their depth will show their seriousness. Should they, however, be faint lines which, while crossing, do not *cut* the line, they will indicate annoying interferences which impede progress. If cutting the line, they are serious checks to the career, and threaten the success, in which case the character of the line after their appearance will show the effect they have produced.

BREAKS are always serious defects to encounter, as they indicate a complete check to the career ; if the line assumes a new character, starting in a new direction, or ending abruptly, they will indicate a total change in the subject's career. If repeatedly broken, there will be a continued succession of reverses, and life will be difficult and troubled. Each break is more or less serious according to the width of the break, and whether it is repaired, while each break is a separate reverse.

With breaks in the lines, it is essential that both hands should be examined in order to ascertain whether all the obstructions form part of the natural plan of the life, as shown in the left hand, or are the result of acquired habits, mistakes in calculations, illness or other causes. It will be found that in by far the larger number of hands, the Line of Saturn is much clearer and better in the left hand than in the right, clearly pointing to the truth that many of our troubles are of our own making. We can and do alter our Fate.

When the line is *uneven*, alternately deep and thin, the periods of prosperity will be intermittent, and the state of affairs will be unreliable and changeable. *A Wavy* line will tell of a constantly changing mode of life, and if with this, the line is uneven or defective, the difficulties in life will be increased.

Commencing deep and clear, at the base of the hand, and reaching to the Mount, it will tell of a prosperous career ; particularly so if there are a number of fine hair-like lines rising upward from it, giving it added strength. But downward lines will detract from its success, and will tell of discouragements which will affect the prosperity.

Should this deep line stop at the Head line, the career of the subject will meet a serious check, either from an error of judgment or misfortune. I have, however, often seen a good line of Saturn thus stopped, but starting again from another point in the Head line—indicating that a new career had been started. The good or poor condition of the new line will indicate the success, but, in any case, the stoppage must be serious, owing to the later age at which the new line commences.

This line is subject to many difficulties in its course, as it will often be seen that many little lines from Mounts Venus and Luna cross the hand and join themselves to the line of Saturn Though no more than worry lines, they are apt to impede the career, especially so with nervous persons whose hands are much rayed and lined. Each of these lines will in some way affect the career, sometimes beneficially, but more often to its detriment.

If this strong deep line runs to the Heart line and then stops, it will indicate misfortune checking the career and arising from disappointment in love—or if the hand is weak, you should suspect heart disease, to ascertain which the Heart and Life lines and nails should be examined.

All lines cutting the Line of Saturn weaken it, and interfere with the success of the subject at the age at which the line is cut. But lines which run alongside, or merge into it, operate to its improvement—to ascertain the nature or cause of this beneficial influence on the career, note well the place from which these lines arise.

If the line of Saturn is thin or defective, and these chance lines (running from all parts of the hand, and representing events or influences which come into or form part of the life) are deep and strong, merging into or running alongside the thin or defective line, it will naturally assist the subject, and considerably strengthen the line of Saturn during their continuance. These lines running alongside act as Sister lines.

The greatest number of defects to this line, as seen in most hands, are to be found in the start of the line—which embraces the earlier years of the life, and discloses the conditions surrounding the starting of the life. It is, however, worthy of note, that these early defective lines usually improve ; the subjects have learnt to avoid difficulties and to help themselves.

On the other hand, those who start with the best lines are apt to meet troubles later, and are frequently found wanting in experience when trying times come, and adversity stares them in the face.

Another usually defective period is that which fills the quadrangle—that is the space between the Head and Heart lines. As a general experience, the years between thirty and forty-five are the most strenuous and most subject to fluctuation. Here, defects are a disaster in proportion as they affect the line. You may see a strong line grow thin as it nears the Head line, while breaks and defects often come. In some hands, the quadrangle is filled with an Island, in which case there will be years of financial difficulties to be encountered.

If this defective portion of the line has a Square repairing the break, the serious set-back will be overcome, and the continuing line will show the result.

If the Line of Saturn at this period of the life is covered with Crosses, it indicates continued reverses which are overcome if the line continues strong. But unless the line does become strong again, the reverses will overcome the subject.

If at any period of its course through the hand, the line is cut by Cross-bars, it will show obstacles affecting the career ; but if the line cuts through the Cross-bars and severs them, then the obstacles will be overcome. A chance line from the Head line cutting the Line of Saturn shows that the difficulties will result from an error of judgment. A similar line from the Heart line will show that the affections have got the better of the subject. A Chance line from Jupiter—particularly if there is a Star on Mount Jupiter—cutting the line, inordinate pride will upset the career. Should this Chance line run to an Island on the Line of Saturn, then the personal ambition will occasion extravagance, ending in serious financial difficulties.

As a general rule, the Line of Saturn always ends on the Mount of Saturn ; but there is one exception to this—it may end on Mount Jupiter, in which case success will be attained through ambition. Lines are often seen branching from the Line of Saturn, and running to one or other of the Mounts. In such cases, the qualities of t he particular Mount will, if the Line of Saturn contin ues good, benefit the career. Thus if such a branch ends in Apollo, success in art, business, or even the stage may be expected; while should this line extend to Mount Mercury, it will add shrewdness, business capability, and give a scientific turn to the mind.

Whenever the condition or character of the line shows that the career is likely to be unsuccessful, the cause of the changing circumstances should be searched for—possibly ill-health, loss of mental power, unhappy or uncongenial surroundings, disease, or disappointment in life, marriage or business, may cause the trouble. Though the Line of Saturn does not itself show ill-health or disease, yet it will show the effects on the career.

The outcome of the career is indicated by the *Termination* of the line. It will be seen that, in some hands, the line does not extend to the Mount of Saturn, but terminates below it. This is not surprising, for the line indicates the duration of productive capability, and it is not unusual in old age, disease or delicacy, that the productiveness of the career should become a negligible quantity.

The absence of a line on the Mount of Saturn would be an indication that there are no forces working against the subject, and if the line is good to its termination, it will tell of productiveness, and an enjoyable old age may be anticipated.

Defective terminations may not mean poverty in old age, or even money losses—they may point to financial checks due to disappointment in children, losses of friends, or other similar troubles. Breaks, Bars cutting the line, Crosses or Dots certainly point to trials, but these often result from ill-health. The line terminating in an Island will tell of financial difficulties in the later days, while if the line has a Cross on the Mount, there will be troubles of all sorts.

Lines coming from Monut Luna or from that direction, whilst indicating the influence of others on the life (as a rule, the opposite sex), are not necessarily love affairs. Unless the Chance line unites with the Line of Saturn, it will have no marked influence on the subject. These Chance lines may touch the Line of Saturn at any point in its course, and the effects can be told from the character of the line after its junction.

In some cases, it may be followed by a break in the line, with overlapping ends, and the appearance of a fine Sister line. In such a case, it may mean marriage—but such a chance line, running for a time alongside the Line of Saturn and then cutting across it, will often show a disappointment, and for a time the line itself will show a defective condition. A double or sister Line of Saturn, if clear and straight, the ends turning towards other Mounts, is an indication of increased influence and importance in life.

THE LINE OF APOLLO
THE LINE OF SUCCESS OR CAPABILITY

This line has no fixed starting point, nor is it to be found in all hands ; but wherever found, it will run toward the Mount of Apollo. It may rise from various points in the hand, such as the Line of Life, the Mount of Luna or the Plain of Mars, sometimes terminating high up on the Mount, and sometimes not reaching the Mount. Whenever it is present, it emphasises the Apollonian traits and qualifications, and indicates a capability or possibility of accomplishing a good deal. Without this

line, the prospects of accomplishing much, however clever or talented, are more or less remote.

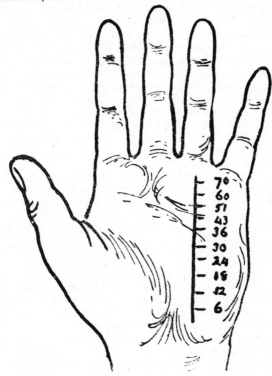

AGE AS SHOWN ON LINE OF APOLLO

The length of the line determines the extent and duration of its influence—the longer the line the more effect it will have, while the shorter the line the less will be its importance.   A line of Apollo, starting from the wrist, running through the hand, and reaching the Mount, will indicate the possession of great talent.   If the line starts low in the hand, and runs only for a short distance, the subject possesses talents but they will not be productive of great results.

If the line rises higher in the hand, and covers the space between the Head and Heart lines (i.e. the Quadrangle), the special talents of the subject will operate during that period. If the line runs on to the Mount, he will be well endued with Apollonian characteristics, and in whichever world he moves, will be brilliant and acquire reputation.

I have often found that the lines of Apollo and Saturn are interdependent ; one will be seen strong at a time when the other is weak. In such cases, they operate upon each other as Sister lines, and the one counteracts the damage to the other. I have invariably found that a good strong line of Apollo will amply compensate for the absence of the line of Saturn. Should the line of Apollo be present and then disappear, afterwards beginning again, the talents of the subject will be latent during the period for which the line if absent—the other lines, if carefully examined, will generally disclose the cause of the break.

When the line of Apollo rises from Upper Mount Luna, it will show that strong imagination is joined to good powers of expression. With such a line, if the mental world was the strongest, I should advise the subject to take up literature, in which success would be attained. If the finger tips are conic and the fingers smooth, then poetry will be the pet ambition ; with knotty fingers and square tips, history or historical novels would be more suitable, while if the Mount of Mars should be large, stories of battles or heroic adventures would accrue therefrom. With the Mount of Venus large, the productions would turn to Nature and the sympathetic. The Mount of Saturn high would show that the subject would write on scientific subjects, chemistry or physics.

This person would, not unlikely, turn out to be an expert writer of weird and uncanny stories. From this example of reading, it is manifest that the Chirognomic Characteristics of the hand practically locate the particular direction in which the line of Apollo will bring success.

Many Palmists, when they see the strong clear line of Apollo, predict unfailing success for their subject, owing to their omission to take into calculation the qualities of the hand in general and the world in which the subject is best suited to operate. A weak thumb, flabby consistency, and a defective Head line would operate seriously and prejudice the line. You will not find many hands with a really good clear line of Apollo marked thereon ; but whenever it is seen, it is of value, other things being equal. In all cases, note the Three Worlds of Palmistry, to determine its application and the tenor of its operation.

The *Character* of the line, its clearness, depth and evenness, will indicate its intensity and the power of the qualities it possesses. The best line is that which is clear, deep, even, well-cut, and without other defects.

A Broad and Shallow line will show that little Apollonian power is present. The subject will be one who will like pretty things, but with a coarse hand, the inclination will be for gaudy and showy things. If, however, the hand is refined, the subject will always dress tastefully, having an eye to the harmony of colourings.

A Chained line is a very undesirable one, as its possessor will be, as to artistic attainments, marked by shallowness, though the subject may be under the delusion that his knowledge is profound. All his artistic efforts will begin and end in talk.

A Wavy line tells of vacillation in the career ; the subject is erratic and unreliable, without doubt clever, and able to do much in his own particular world of operation, but too prone to go off at a tangent and waste his talents, instead of concentrating in one direction. The final result will be most uncertain. Should the line, however, straighten on the Mount, the ultimate prospects will be more encouraging, especially if it terminates in a star.

This line, as is the case with the other lines, is subject to defects, and one of the most serious is the Island. When seen on a deep line, it will indicate that the realisation of wealth and fame will meet a serious check—not only so, but actual loss of money and reputation may be experienced. Whichever may be the world in which he moves, things promising to result well will be attempted, but they will end in failure and loss.

If the finger of Apollo is as long as, or longer than the finger of Saturn, he will be a plunger and will take desperate chances to win—given the third phalanx of the finger of Apollo long and thick, he will be a gambler.

With the finger of Mercury crooked and twisted, you will have the card-sharper and trickster, one who is not above resorting to cheating, and who uses the brilliancy of the line of Apollo to serve his ends. In any hand, no matter how good, the presence of an Island is a warning which must not be unregarded.

Bars cutting the line show constant impediments to success. These bars arise from various causes and they may generally be located by chance lines, the Mounts, or Influence lines. If these bars cut the line, the career will be affected ; but if they are only minute lines, they will tell of annoying interferences which cause constant worry, and retard progress. Dots when seen on the line are a menace to the reputation, and if they are large and deep, indicate the actual loss of good name.

Breaks in the line indicate set-backs to the career and ambitions ; not only do they impede progress but destroy the usefulness of the line and render it inoperative. In all cases of breaks, look carefully for any repair signs calculated to remedy the defect ; but even repaired lines are no more than equal to a broad and shallow line.

As with the other lines, it is the termination which tells the result of its operation. If it ends in a Dot it points to a loss of reputation, the career ending in disgrace. Ending in a Star, it will indicate brilliant success. If the life's operations have been in the mental world, renown will have been attained as a poet, writer, painter, sculptor, actor, in or some artistic profession. If the life has been spent in the practical world, then money has been made with ease and rapidity. Ending as it occasionally does in a double Star, then dazzling brilliancy and great fame will result. In some hands a Star may be seen lower down the line, as well as at its termination ; in such cases the first or lower Star will indicate the age at which success has been achieved, while the terminating Star indicates that the success attained will continue to the end of the life.

A deep Bar terminating the line, points to some insurmountable obstruction arising near the close of the life. With this defect, if the Life line at about the age of fifty years shows defects, then ill-health or delicacy will ruin the career. The Head and Heart lines should also be examined for defective markings.

For the line to terminate in a Cross is an even worse defect than a Bar, as it means an absolute blemish to the reputation. It will also indicate serious want of judgment, and points to one who will make frequent mistakes in the course of his life, which will in consequence end very unfavourably.

The line terminating in a Square is a favourable marking, and indicates protection from all defects of the line throughout life. An Island at the termination is a very unfavourable indication, as no matter how good, deep or clear the line may be throughout its course, this marking will tell of the life finishing under a heavy cloud, including loss of money and reputation.

The line may often be seen terminating in a Fork. This tells of one who is talented in more than one direction, but that this diversity of gifts will cause him to do less than he could do if his efforts were more concentrated. Should the line terminate in a well-marked Trident. it is nearly as promising as a Star, for it tells of wealth and celebrity achieved through mental efforts.

If on the Mount two parallel lines are seen, one on each side of the Line of Apollo, they will give added strength to an already strong line. Should there be several vertical lines on the Mount, it will tell of a diversity too widespread to admit of success, and will be about equal to a Tassel.

The line may at its termination branch off to Mount Saturn or to Mount Mercury, thus giving to the line the combined wisdom (Saturn), brilliancy (Apollo) and shrewdness (Mercury) ; the result will be wealth and reputation.

All branches or fine lines *rising* from the line itself increase the beneficial effects of the line, if good, and go to make success the more assured. But the lines falling from the line indicate the necessity of greater and more concentrated efforts to assure success.

Branch lines running from the line towards other lines, signs or Mounts, will each have a special and distinct meaning ; this can be ascertained from the place at which such branch lines terminate. Such a branch line, for instance, running to Mount Mercury will bring the shrewdness of Mercury to the assistance of the subject. If Stars are on the Mounts of Mercury and Apollo, the success will be intensified ; but crosses, bars, dots, or other defects will tell of costly mistakes.

The Line of Apollo does not apply to Art only, but to every class of daily occupation. It tells of possibilities which can be achieved in some direction, which will be disclosed by the general characteristics of the hands.

Influence lines running from Mount Venus alongside the line, will show that the assistance of relatives has aided success. Should, however, a line from the Heart line cut the line, it will show that an affection will interfere with the success.

By noting the line throughout its course, as well as its variations in character, depth and clearness and each defect, together with all chance lines which merge into it, cut or run alongside it, and noting the source of each of these chance lines and their respective qualities as helps or hindrances to the line, you will be able to reason out any formation of the Line of Apollo which can possibly occur.

THE LINE OF MERCURY

OR LINE OF HEALTH

This line should start on Mount Luna and run upwards, on the percussion of the hand, to the Mount of Mercury, from which Mount it derives its name. It is a valuable line, as it affords an indication of the condition of the digestive organs, and in conjunction with the Line of Life, Saturn and Apollo, it is especially important as a guide to business success, owing to its health indications.

Although this line should rise from Mount Luna, I have found in my own practice that it rarely does so. In the majority of hands, it wil be found rising from towards the Lines of Saturn or Life, sometimes from the base or centre of the hand, and often in the Plain of Mars. When rising from the Line of Life, it tells but too surely of heart weakness—not necessarily disease. This marking should be of peculiar interest to the Medical Profession, as it reveals tendencies that the stethoscope may fail to disclose.

To afford the best promise of success, this line should not at any point in its course touch the Line of Life. The

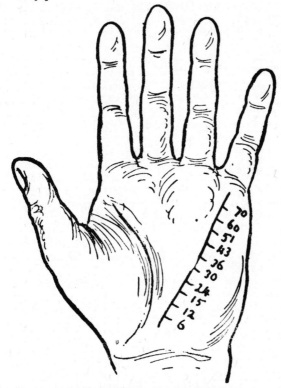

TIME SHOWN ON LINE OF MERCURY

source of the line, either outside and apart from the Line of Life, is immaterial.

The presence of a really good, clear, deep-cut and well coloured line is rarely seen, especially after the subject has passed the stage of youth. In many hands the line may be entirely absent; this indicates a person who, other things being equal, will be vivacious, quick in manner and speech, not knowing anything of liver trouble, and to whom life is indeed worth living.

The Character of the line is of primary importance, as a deep and clear line of Mercury not only indicates a good constitution and strong vitality, but also a clear brain and a good memory. A good Head line will be much disturbed, and its operations impeded, by a poor line of Mercury.

Given a hand with good and clear lines of Life, Head and Heart, a line of Mars, and a deep clear line of Mercury, and you have one who will virtually never experience a day's sickness. If such a hand is bad in its chirognomic aspect, the strong condition of health will add intensity to the passions and appetite, and from this type the criminal class and drunkards are recruited.

The mere thinness of the line does not lessen its influence ; it still gives support from a good operation of the liver, though not so strongly as a deep line. In all estimates of the Line of Mercury, the general proportion of the line, when compared with the other lines of the hand, must be borne in mind, for a normal balance is the best.

The line being Broad and Shallow will tell of one not over strong, and any severe tax on the stomach will cause disarrangement.

The line being Chained shows a diseased liver and stomach. This defect must not be confused with an Island—chaining must consist of short loops, and is one of the worst formations. The subject is always a sufferer, and such a condition always spells poor success in business.

The length of the line adds materially to its power and usefulness. If a long line is also a good one, its influence means good health and success during life. If, however, it is defective, then look for ill-health and indifferent success in all undertakings.

The defects in this line are of a similar nature to those found in the other lines, as regards being thick or thin or chained, and bear the same construction as to their operation.

Whenever the line is seen to be Wavy, it will indicate that the subject is a sufferer from chronic biliousness ;

in many cases there may often be a complication of rheumatism with biliousness—anyhow, the indications for rheumatism should be verified.

Should the line present a Ladder-like appearance, it will indicate that the subject is a victim to the worst stomach trouble—dyspepsia, gastric fever, catarrh of the stomach or the intestines, or inflammation of the bowels may be experienced.

Dots on the line serve to indicate acute attacks of bilious or stomach trouble at the age indicated. Chance lines from these Dots to health defects, or lines on the Mounts, should be noted carefully. If with a Dot, the line is broken or otherwise defective on the Mount of Mercury, you will know that a severe attack of bilious or gastric fever has occurred at the age at which the Dot is seen on the line. This method of examination should be observed as to the other lines and Mounts, whenever Dots are seen on the line.

Cross-bars may be seen cutting the line, evidencing illness at the age at which they are seen. The extent to which they cut the line will show the severity of the attack—the nature of the illness being indicated on the other lines or Mounts. In all cases of variation in this line, or any defect in it, the Head line should be examined.

Islands are frequently seen on the line ; as in the case of the Line of Life, they indicate delicacy of the health during the period for which it is present. The cause can be located in the usual way. It must, however, be noted that the detrimental effects of an Island on the line are not always confined to stomach or liver disorders, but will apply equally to other illnesses. Should the line be found to be Islanded throughout its whole course, or showing two or more fair-sized Islands, it will indicate that the throat and lungs are delicate. In such cases Grilles or Cross-bars will be seen on the Upper Mount of Mars, or the nails will be bulbous.

Breaks often occur in the line and are indications of health trouble ; if it is continuously broken, it will tell of delicacy of the stomach. These broken lines are at times seen with repair signs—of these, the most effective and beneficial is the Square. When the line runs deeply on to the Mount of Mercury and branches rise from it, the subject will not only possess good health, but will also be successful in business. In all instances, it is essential to place the subject in his proper World, as indicated by the phalanges of the Mercury finger, as success cannot be so certainly predicted if the subject is out of his true sphere of operations.

As with the other lines, it is the termination of the line which will furnish the outcome of the career, and in this respect its form of termination should be treated in much the same way as that of the other lines.

Note, however, that when the line terminates in a Grille, there will be little success experienced, owing to ill-health or dishonesty. In such a case, the lines and hand must be noted carefully to ascertain which is the fault.

A Star terminating the line will tell of certain success in the particular world indicated by the fingers ; while with good lines of Saturn and Apollo, the force of the Star will be assured.

As a matter of fact, in all readings of the Line of Mercury, it is advisable to take all the lines, as well as the type of the subject into consideration, and particularly the Lines of Head and Life, as in all the walks of life, brains and health are necessary to success, and cannot be dispensed with—hence every change or defect in the character of this line is important in its bearing upon health or business success.

There is occasionally to be seen a Star on this line, at the point at which it crosses the Line of Head. When this is seen in a woman's hand, it will indicate either serious female trouble, or that the subject will have a trying and dangerous time in child-birth.

CHAPTER VIII

In addition to the Main lines, there are at times other lines to be seen in the hand that are fairly clear and well-cut, and too strong to be classed among the fine lines known as Chance lines. Thus they form a class of their own, not so important as the Main ones, yet often exercising marked influence for good or evil on the operations of the principal lines, and also influencing the character of the subject. They are classified as Minor lines, and their effect must be noted in order to determine rightly the operation of the Main lines.

VIA LASCIVIA

This line is seldom seen in the hand, but when present it should run in such a way as to form itself into a Sister line to the Line of Mercury. Generally it occupies a slanting position, rises from the inside of the base of Mount Luna, and as a rule terminates on the lower part of Upper Mount Luna. It probably received its name from the fact that, given a strong line of Mercury with this as a Sister line, it would largely increase the Vitality, giving an added force to the ardour and energy in all the pursuits of life. It does not necessarily indicate sensuality, unless the type of the hand in which it is seen is sensual—in other cases the superfluous energy would be expended in work.

In any case, if found deep and clearly marked, it will tend to lower its possessor in some way—if the hand containing it is a soft pleasure-loving one, with Mount Venus full, then the subject will be a devotee to pleasure, without regard to expense or consequences—branches running from the line, if any, will show the results of excess if leading to defects.

133

When clear, deep and unbroken, and running parallel with the line of Mercury, fully on to the Mount of Mercury, it is an indication of good success arising from eloquence and talent ; if it has a fine line running from it to the line to Apollo, then wealth may be predicted.

If the line is uneven or twisted, it will tell of cunning and unfaithfulness in all things—the type of the subject must be considered in order to determine the effect of this line. In a low animal hand, this line is a menace and a warning of excess ; but in a fine and high-minded type, the line should be taken as an indication of conscientious work and fine results.

THE GIRDLE OF VENUS

This line, as a rule, rises between the fingers of Jupiter and Saturn, and runs in a semi-circle under the Mounts of Saturn and Apollo, ending between the fingers of Apollo and Mercury. It may also take its rise on the Mount of Jupiter, ending on Mount Mercury, or even at times extending to the percussion. It is, in part, a sister line to the Heart line, and in some cases when the Heart line is absent it takes its place.

This line is a subject of much misconception ; many Palmists regard it as a menace to the morality of its possessor, but my experience confirms me in the belief that its presence does not as a rule indicate immorality or licentiousness, but that in the majority of cases it indicates a highly sensitive and nervous subject. If the hand is a weak one, expect hysteria.

It is by no means an uncommon sign, being seen frequently in hands of all types. In many instances of hands which contain the Girdle, the palm will be crossed by many fine lines, running in all directions, which in itself is an added confirmation of an intensely nervous temperament.

On hands showing but a few lines, giving a phlegmatic temperament, the Girdle is of little importance as an indication of nerves. But if the hand is coarse and sensual, with Mount Venus excessive and red, animal in its composition, then the Girdle may be read as an added force to the animal propensities. In an ordinary hand, it not only improves it, but indicates ardour and enthusiasm and sharpens the intellect.

When crossed by many fine lines, and with the Mounts of Venus and Luna highly developed, an hysterical tendency is indicated. If the Girdle cuts the lines of Saturn and Apollo, it will indicate an obstacle to success— generally caused by some outburst of temper or petulance or some love affair.

If the line extends further across the hand than between the fingers of Apollo and Mercury, so much the better, as it opens the way for the extra force derived from Mount Mercury, and will help largely in commercialism. If cut on Mount Apollo by a line other than the line of Apollo, it will tell of loss of fortune or reputation by folly or dissipation.

If it should be composed of a double or triple line then its indication, whether of health or temperament, will be increasingly strong. If composed of a number of broken lines, the hand being in other respects a nervous one, the danger from hysteria is great. With such a marking, the lines of Life and Head will often be found defective, while defects in the lines of Saturn and Apollo may be sufficiently accounted for by a broken Girdle of Venus. Should the line of Head slope low on Mount Luna, while on it or near its termination is seen a Star, Cross, Island or Dot, with a broken Girdle, and the hand is crossed by innumerable fine lines, there will be danger of insanity, or even self-destruction, from uncontrolled nerves.

The Girdle of Venus is seen in many hands and in all types ; many of the best and finest men and women have it, and their careers have never suffered in the slightest by reason of it. All that is necessary in reading the Girdle is to fit it to the type of your subject, and not fit the subject to the line. The Girdle is not evil in itself, but it can operate to accentuate evil when it exists in a militant form.

THE LINE OF INTUITION

This line, when present, lies at the side of the hand near the percussion. It rises on Mount Luna, curves inwards towards the palm, and ends on or near Mount Mercury.

Its position is near the line of Mercury, but its distinguishing feature lies in its decided curve.

The presence of this line, if well and clearly marked, adds greatly to the intuitive faculties, and tends to increase the Mercurian keenness. Its possessors receive impressions for which they cannot account, and are given to form opinions which are accurate, though they are quite unable to give any reasons for such opinions. I have found it result in increased sensitiveness and added keenness in estimating the characters of people. Many are not conscious of the possession of such faculties, but with this marking they *feel* things, though why they do so they are quite at a loss to say.

In judging the effect or power of this line, regard must be had to the character of the hand in which it is found. In a hand which is hard, with square fingers and tips, and with but few lines on it, the intuition afforded by the line will be passed over as foolish. But with long fingers, pointed tips, Mount Luna full, the Head line sloping, the subject will be strongly psychic and will dream dreams, have visions, strong presentiments of danger—in fact, the subject is one before whom coming events will cast their shadows, and they will be strong believers in signs and omens. This sign or line I have often seen in the hands of Clairvoyants and Spiritualist Mediums.

A deep, clear line will give the greatest amount of intuition, whilst if broken or otherwise defective, it will limit its effectiveness. An Island on the line will indicate that the intuitiveness resulting from the line will bring little success.

A branch line running from a deep clear line of Intuition to Mount Jupiter, will indicate that the subject will be very ambitious to use such intuitions to the best advantage; such a person would be likely to make his or her mark in occultism. A rising line to the Mount of Apollo will tell of a measure of renown arising through the full use of the intuition; but a line rising from this marking and cutting through the line of Saturn, will show that the exercise of the intuitive faculties will seriously prejudice the career. However, should this rising line merge into the line of Saturn, it will benefit the career.

At times this line of Intuition may be found mixed up with a defective line of Mercury ; in such a case any exercise of the intuitive faculties will prejudice the health, and particularly affect the nervous system to its disadvantage. Such subjects would be well advised to leave psychic matters severely alone.

As a general rule the marking is a great help to any hand, but it requires commonsense to regulate its operations.

THE LINE OF MARS

This is a line which rises on the Lower Mount of Mars, and runs very close to but inside the line of Life. It is, in fact, a Sister line to it, and must lie very close to it. Its presence in the hand assures a stronger constitution to its possessor than even that indicated by a deep, clear and well-cut line of Life. But it must be considered in connection with the line of Life and the type of the subject. Should the line of Life be marked by defects, with the line of Mars present, the person will be subject to delicacy, but there will be an underlying strength which will operate to prevent serious trouble being experienced. This added vitality will, if the line extends the full length of the line of Life, continue throughout the life ; but if only existing during a portion of the line of Life, its influence will be marked for the period indicated.

Lines rising from the line of Mars, if crossing the line of Life, indicate a tendency to rise in life, due to increased physical ardour. If such a rising line reaches to and merges into the line of Head, it will occasion increased mental force as an additional aid to success—a similar result will accrue should such rising line merge in the line of Saturn.

It is essential, with this line present, to note carefully the type of the subject and the general character of the hand, for if the hand is sensual, the line of Life strong, deep and clear, with Mount Venus large, then (with the line of Mars clear) you will have one who will be prone to excessive indulgence of the sexual appetites, which will need an unusually deep and clear line of Head and a strong Thumb to restrain.   With such a hand, if a line from the line of Mars runs to and cuts the line of Apollo, or the line of Saturn, it will indicate that such excessive indulgence has interfered with the career.   If the line of Apollo terminates in a Dot, Bar or Cross, then the subject will also suffer a loss of reputation.   If such rising line, in such a hand, cuts a line of affection, then the domestic life of the subject will be ruined by excess.

I have seen instances where a line of Mars has run well down towards the base of the hand, then has taken a turn, and, cutting through the line of Life, ran across the hand and terminated upon the Mount of Luna.   This indicates such an excess of vitality that the usual length of the life does not afford sufficient scope for its expenditure, so an outlet is found in other directions—often in drunkenness and debauchery, with great restlessness.   In others, the excess of energy will find an outlet in travel and licentiousness.   If the line ends in a dot, star, cross or bar, the subject, after a life of excess, will die suddenly ; but with a star at the termination of the Head line, loss of reason will result.

The line of Mars in itself is a good indication, but there is always a measure of danger of excess, unless other indications to balance it are present.   In a good hand, its presence adds power and ability to achieve success, though it tends to produce hastiness of temper and excitability.

THE RING OF SOLOMON

This sign is rarely seen in hands.   It is formed by a continuation of the line of Heart which, instead of rising on Mount Jupiter, curls around the finger of Jupiter in form of a ring.   It is usually seen on the hands of females. Its presence indicates the possession of Psychic and Occult powers, and its possessor will undoubtedly have good capacity for Clairvoyance, Palmistry, and even Mesmerism, according to the type of the hand and the general intelligence.   When the sign is seen in a man's hand, it will make him very fastidious, extremely sensitive, and difficult to understand.

THE RING OF SATURN

This sign varies in its appearance, sometimes rising between the fingers of Jupiter and Saturn, forming a complete circle, and terminating between the fingers of Saturn and Apollo ; in many hands it is composed of two lines, which cross each other on Mount Saturn.

It is an unfavourable marking, inasmuch as it indicates a disposition to change from one occupation to another, without remaining at one thing long enough to ensure any success.   There will be a want of continuity of purpose, and a consequent failure to achieve success.   Cutting the Mount of Saturn, it operates as an actual defect.

If the Ring is broken, so that it does not completely encircle the Mount, the effect is less serious.   In any and every case, the Ring must be read as a warning of danger; to overcome the vacillation and changeableness, and to lessen the operation of this Sign, a strong will and a good line of Head are essential.

The Sign fortunately is not often seen in the hand—but when present it will account for many defects in the lines of Saturn and Apollo.

LINES OF AFFECTION OR MARRIAGE

The lines of Marriage, as they are usually but erroneously termed, are to be found on the Mount of Mercury ; they run from the percussion toward the centre of the Mount.   In some hands a number of these lines are to be seen ; others contain none ; they have always been considered as indications of marriage by the old-time Palmists, but experience proves that as absolute indications of marriage, they are woefully misleading.

They are frequently seen on the hands of persons who have never married, hence their uncertainty as marriage lines.   They should properly be termed lines of Affection and indicate the number of persons who have made a deep impression on the life ; as a rule they refer to the opposite sex outside the subject's own family, though occasionally I have seen indicated in this way a very strong affection between two members of a family, when one (or both) was married.

To determine the age at which such an affection occurs,

the space between the Heart line and the top of Mount Mercury must be divided into the average years of life. Thus, the middle of Mount Mercury would indicate thirty-six years, while the top of the Mount would be about seventy years, taking the Heart line as the starting point—this method of determining the age I have always found reliable. The length and depth of the lines show the strength and duration of the affection.

If many lines of Affection are seen on the hand, it will indicate that the subject is very susceptible in affairs of the heart—in fact, very much of a flirt. In such cases, the strength of the affection will be indicated by the strength or weakness of the lines.

When the lines of Affection are thinner than the other lines in the hand, it will indicate that the subjects have no really strong affection and are undemonstrative in their affections. Should the line start deep and strong and then grow thin and weak, the affection will weaken.

These lines, as is the case with the other lines in the hand, are subject to obstacles. Thus, a Cross on a line of Affection will indicate a serious obstacle to the affections, while a Star will tell of a total breach. A Break will show an interference in the course of the affection ; a Fork at the end of the line will tell of separation, and, with other indications, of divorce.

A branching or turning of the line of Affection towards the Heart line, will indicate the death of the person loved, and often from the point where the line of Affection touches the Heart line, a fine line will run to a point in the Life line, which will indicate the date when such an event will happen. Drooping branches from the line of Affection will indicate much sorrow and disappointment in married life.

Too much care cannot be taken in dealing with these lines of Affection ; it is essential to take into consideration the indications of marriage to be found in other parts of the hand. The lines of Life and Saturn will generally afford a more reliable ground for predicting marriage. Often the Life line will show a break and a change in the line, when the character of the line after the break will show whether such change has been or will be beneficial or otherwise.   In addition, it frequently occurs that a new line of influence starts from such a break and runs inside the Life line and close to it.   If such an influence line, after running for a space close to the Life line, widens out from it, it will tell of a want of sympathy or closeness on the part of the influence.

As regards the indications of marriage on the Line of Saturn, they will be found in lines from Mount Luna joining the line of Saturn, which invariably indicate an influence joining the life—the subsequent character of the line of Saturn will show the purpose of the influence on the life.   Lines from Mount Luna coming to but not joining the line of Saturn, will be but transient influences—but should the line cross the line of Saturn, it will tell of an influence crossing the life.   If at the point of crossing, a hollow is shown on the hand, a disappointment will have been experienced ; following this hollow, the line of Saturn will often be defective for a period.

SIGNS OF WIDOWHOOD.   A break in the line of Affection indicates the sudden death of the partner ; when the line of Affection, after going straight for a time and without breaking, turns down to and touches the Heart line ; when the line of Affection is cut at its termination by another line ; by the line of Affection terminating in a Star on Mount Mercury.   As to whether these signs relate to a past or future event, the age at which the event is noted should be ascertained, while the lines of Life Heart, and Saturn should be examined for indications of change or shock at the age corresponding with that of the sign on the marriage line.

PHYSICAL INCAPACITY is often indicated by the line of Life lying very close on Mount Venus.   The lines of Head and Mercury being joined together by a Star will in addition constitute a strong indication of sterility. A Cross on the third phalange of a woman's hand is often an indication of sterility.   In addition to these I have found that when evidence of female weakness is to be seen on Lower Mount Luna, or on the line of Mercury, together with an upward rising of the centre of the First Rascette (or bracelet), there is likely to be sterility.   As a pre-marital indication this should be valuable.

THE RASCETTES

The Rascettes or Bracelets are the lines which cross the wrist. In many hands there are three, but in others there may be only two and in some but one. Beyond the first one I have found them of little use.

In my experience I have not found them useful as an indication of longevity, hence the old-time tradition of ascribing thirty years of life for each of the Rascettes is fallacious. I have seen subjects over eighty years of age with only two Rascettes, while I have known of others with three well-formed and clear lines who died young.

The first Rascette, if deep and clear, will add confirmation to other indications in the hand of the possession of a strong constitution ; doubtless it will add strength to a long, clear and deep Life line. Should, however, the Rascette be poorly marked, be broad and shallow or chained, the contitution will be weak. These Rascettes should be considered with the Life line. The rising of the centre of the first Rascette towards the palm I have already instanced as a pre-marital indication, in part, of sterility.

Long branches from the Rascette, rising high into the Mount of Luna, are known as travel lines, and are read to indicate voyages ; should such a line run to the Mount of Jupiter, the voyage will be a long and happy one. A Star at the termination of a voyage line is usually read as death by drowning.

These lines are found marked with similar defects as the other lines, and this indicates troubles en route.

In addition to these indications of travel I have invariably found that when the Life line sweeps out in the hand towards the Mount of Luna, the subject either has or will spend some years in another and generally distant country. If such a Life line should be long, reaching nearly to the centre of the Rascette, the change will result in lengthening materially the duration of the life.

A straight line from the Rascette to Mount Mercury indicates a sudden and unexpected increase of the finances; a similar line rising to and joining the line of Saturn will indicate the return of a friend from across the water.

THE QUADRANGLE

This is the space lying between the lines of Heart and Head; it reaches across the hand from between the fingers of Jupiter and Saturn to the Mount of Luna. It should be fairly wide at both ends, but not too narrow in the centre, and also clear of lines other than the lines of Saturn, Apollo and Mercury. It will then indicate one who is, other things being equal, faithful, loyal, and of an equable temperament. When too narrow in the centre, it will tell of one capable of being unjust and often avaricious. Should the Quadrangle be narrow under Mount Mercury, it will indicate one who is unduly anxious in respect to his reputation.

When too wide throughout, it will tell of folly and imprudence, notwithstanding any indications of prudence in other parts of the hand. Should the Quadrangle be much lined with fine lines, it will tell of nervous irritability.

The "Croix Mystique," if present, will usually be found under or near the finger of Saturn, in which position, if well and clearly defined, it will indicate a capability for the occult. Badly formed, it is an indication of misfortune. Sometimes a well-formed Star may be seen in the Quadrangle, and it is an indication of trustworthiness ; its fortunate possessors usually attain to financial success by merit.

Chance Lines. In many hands a large number of lines are found crossing the palms in every direction ; these consist of Chance lines and Worry lines of all descriptions, and every line which is not one of the main or minor lines will belong to this class of line.

Hands thus crossed with a multiplicity of lines belong to persons who are extremely nervous, and given to entertaining emotions and ideas of all kinds. These lines, however, are not of much value, unless they occasion defects in the Main lines of the hand—in general, they are best regarded as merely indicating extreme nervousness.

Some of these chance lines will be seen to begin on one Mount and terminate on another, showing some connection between the respective qualities of the Mounts ;

these will have a definite, and often an important meaning.

Occasionally they may start from a Main or a Minor line and terminate on a Mount, or another Main or Minor line. Thus from an Affection line which slopes towards the Heart line, a fine Chance line may often be seen running across the palm to the Life line, and indicating the death of the marriage partner at the time or age at which it touches the Life line.

Chance lines from the percussion across Mount Luna will tell of health trouble peculiar to the portion of the Mount from which they originate, while the point at which they touch the Life line will give the age. Often a number of small lines from Mount Venus, cutting the Life line, indicate worries from friends ; a Chance line from the Life line to Mount Venus, terminating in a Star, will tell of the sudden death of a relative.

These instances are not mentioned as being in any way a full list of Chance or Worry lines, but only as an illustration as to how such lines are dealt with in actual practice, and the method adopted in reading them.

CHAPTER IX

THE PROFESSIONS

It is impossible to be certain, from the hand, what profession or occupation your subject may follow—but the type of hand will show you for what walk in life he or she is best fitted. That is as far as you can go. I give herewith a number of typical hands, taken from life, with an indication of the profession for which the person was *best suited*. They must tell their own story.

Business Hand : Thumb large and long—line of Head straight, finger tips square, with Mercury Mount well developed, and Mercury finger long and square.

Accountant : Mount of Mercury strong—good line of Apollo and Saturn—Second Knots well developed, and strong Thumb.

Architect : Square fingers—a good line of Apollo, and a good line of Saturn—with Mount Mercury strong.

The Law : A good finger of Jupiter—Mounts of Jupiter and Mercury well developed—Thumb turned out with its second phalanx long and broad, and first phalanx of Mercury long—good lines of Head, Saturn and Apollo.

Solicitor : Tips square. Two knots on fingers—medium-sized hands—nails inclined to be short and broad, with Saturn finger and Mount well developed. Thumb strong, Mercury finger and Mount strong.

The Navy : Hand generally as Army, with the addition of a strong Luna, and the Line of Life spreading well out into the palm at its base—showing travel by water.

The Army : The hand large, strong Thumb, with first phalanx well developed—the Mounts of Mars high—good lines of Saturn and Apollo, with square or spatulate Tips—fingers normal length.

The Clergy : A good first finger, Mount of Jupiter well developed, also Mounts Venus and Luna—Head line slightly drooping to Luna—Finger of Mercury long and straight, with first phalanx pointed, and Mount Mercury fairly high.

Doctor : Mount Mercury rayed vertically—the line of Apollo clearly defined—with spatulate fingers and hard hands, the surgeon is indicated—the fingers are usually long, with knots of order developed, and in both types, Luna should be strong.

Artist : The peculiarities of these are as varied as the styles of paintings—with long, square-tipped, and knotted fingers, we have the Artist who revels too much in detail.

Pointed smooth fingers will depict the ideal in Art—but in all, the Mount of Apollo is strongly developed, and also Mount Jupiter.

Sculptor : The fingers usually are more or less spatulate—the lines few in number, the Mounts of Venus, Mars and Luna are high, the hand thick and strong, palm broad.

Musician : Saturn finger long, with Mount Saturn fully developed—fingers long for stringed instruments or short for keys, but in both the fingers are supple for performers—Square and knotty fingers for composers—Spatulate for executants—Mounts of Apollo and Venus well developed. *Vocalist* : Fingers short, smooth or mixed type—all the finger Mounts well developed, and Mount Venus largely prominent—hand soft and plump.

Actor : Long flexible fingers, smooth. Apollo finger spatulate—Mounts of Venus and Luna prominent. Head line drooping to Luna, and the first phalanx of Mercury long. The line of Head turned up towards the Mount of Mercury.

Literary Hand : The Mounts of Jupiter and Luna should be prominent, with long finger of Apollo—Tips spatulate or square, with full knotted second joints. *Literary Critics* have as a rule short nails, and Mount Mercury is prominent—*Poetical*, large Mounts Luna and Venus, with Head line sloping towards Luna—fingers smooth and pointed.

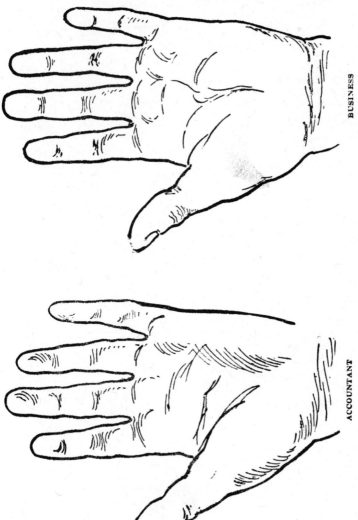

BUSINESS

ACCOUNTANT

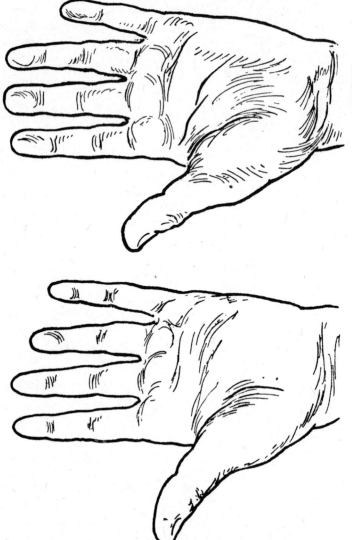

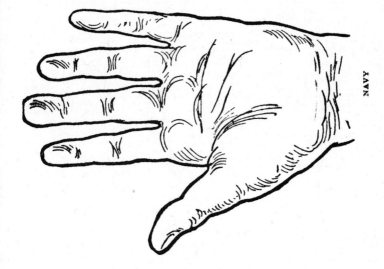

NAVY

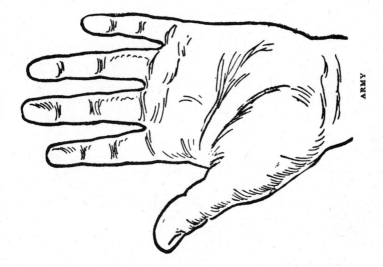

ARMY

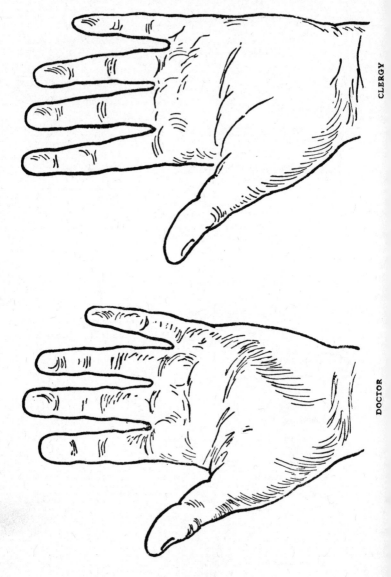

CLERGY

DOCTOR

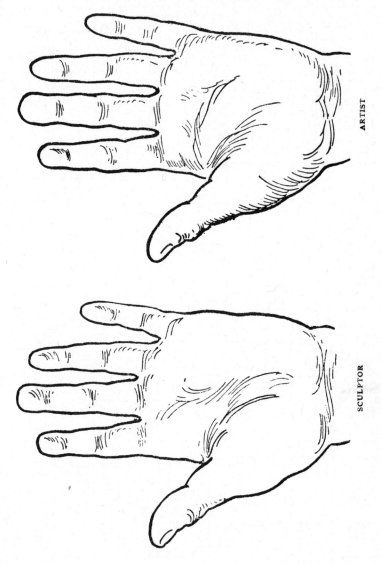

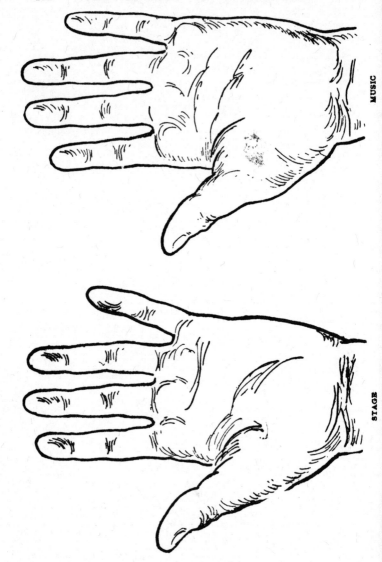

MUSIC

STAGE

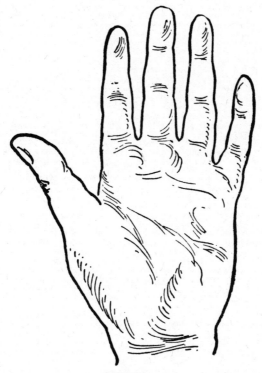

LITERARY

CHAPTER X

In the years during which I have practised as a Professional Palmist, I have inspected many a thousand pair of hands, and heard many an objection raised against the Science. I have invariably found such objectors to be ignorant even of the fact that their own hands were not alike. The mere pointing out of one or two variations has sent them adrift on the ocean of speculation.

To one such objector I said, "Show me your hands, both of them." He held them out and a cursory glance was sufficient for my purpose. Taking only the finger of Jupiter in each hand, I saw that in the left hand the finger was pointed and only of medium length, whilst that in the right was broader in the tip and longer. I then said to him : "In your earlier years, you were not only fervently religious in your aspirations, but were easily influenced, aye, even led by your religious teachers. To-day finds you less credulous, less religious, less docile, and far more ready to accept responsibility." The accuracy of this simple reading was admitted, and he went so far as to admit that he was puzzled, and thought that there might be something after all in Palmistry.

To enable my readers to use the information contained in this book in such a way as to deepen their own interest in the Science, while interesting others, the following points on the individual fingers may be welcome—but due regard must be paid to the whole hand, as laid down in the earlier chapters.

JUPITER : If long this finger shows pride and contemplation ; if very long, however, it indicates a sense of luxury, love of pleasure and comfort, combined with arrogance and egoism.

If short, it indicates activity and impulse, and a

tendency to avoid responsibility. If very short a dislike for responsibility and incapability of undertaking it.

Long and Pointed, it betrays religious instincts and inclinations, together with pride and strong ambition. With the second phalanx long, the ambition will be strong, while the third phalanx long betrays pride and a love of rule. Long and Square, there will be a love of and search for truth from natural sources of information, and a desire to get to the bottom of things.

If Spatulate, there will be much of originality, with intense mysticism ; while if the fingers are smooth, error is indicated.

CONIC TIP : This will add idealistic and intuitive qualities.

SQUARE TIP : This gives commonsense views ; such a subject will reason and take less for granted ; will love landscape painting.

SPATULATE TIP : This will give agnosticism, originality ; such a person will follow no church or creed, and will manifest a domineering spirit, such as marks the tyrant and despot. The broader the tip the more dominating the trend, and the less religious.

2ND PHALANX : Tells of ambition and practical matters.

If Tip is Conic, add Conic qualities.

If Square, it will afford the best indication for business.

If Spatulate, an active, ambitious, original subject, who will force his way through the world.

3RD PHALANX : This is most important, as when long and not thick, it shows that the lower world is normal and supports the upper phalanx. If this phalanx is very much longer than the other two, then the ambition and desire to rule is sordid, not refined. If it is long and thick, gluttony must be added, or (as I have frequently found in practice) in a woman's hand, the thick long third phalanx will show the capable cook. If the phalanx is waist-like and long, gluttony will be absent, higher ideals will hold sway and health defects go. The health trouble will be the nerves, throat or lungs. If the phalanx is flabby, it will indicate a ruined stomach and dyspepsia.

SATURN : The First phalanx longest indicates the Student thinker, inclined to be superstitious and fond of the occult.

2ND PHALANX longest. Farming, agricultural, scientific investigations, chemistry, history or physics will attract.

3RD PHALANX longest. Money worship, or if the type of subject is good, economical. If coarse or bad, miserliness. If thick, less studious. If waist-like, fond of study. If the fingers are bent, it will give added shrewdness.

If the finger is short : balance and seriousness will be entirely lacking, while with a Spatulate tip, there will be no stamina.

If Saturn only has a Conic tip, it will weaken the balance of the character. If Pointed, it will indicate idealism and rampant superstition ; the subject will be ruled by dreams, signs and omens, and the more certainly so if the first phalanx is long.

The Square tip will give practical commonsense and more of soberness ; but if very square, there will be a tendency to melancholy.

The Spatulate tip will add acitivity and originality and gives greater seriousness.

APOLLO : The First phalanx longest shows that Artistic mental qualities are strongest, and indicates the Artist, Writer or Poet.

2ND PHALANX longest, the business side will be uppermost.

3RD PHALANX longest, not destined for art ; there will be a love of display, the taste will be common, with a marked liking for showy colours.

With the First and Second phalanges equal, the artistic talents will be used to make money. The Second phalanx short may secure reputation, but no money.

The Second and Third phalanges equal in length, and long, the desire to make money will be strong, but no artistic qualities will be present.

CONIC TIP will make the subject more artistic, and with a long first phalanx, the qualities will be enhanced; with the Second phalanx longest, the artistic qualities will be applied to business.

SQUARE TIP makes the subject more practical and regular in his habits. It gives commonsense, and practical ideas are added to good business qualities. With the Third phalanx longest, there will be a strong desire for riches, and when obtained a great show of wealth would be made in a vulgar ostentatiousness.

SPATULATE TIP adds activity and originality, and also dramatic ability, marking a natural entertainer. All the qualities of pleasure-giving are marked by originality and activity, often producing a clever after-dinner speaker and mimic. With the Third phalanx longest, there will be not only a fondness for games, but much skill and dash in them. Knotty fingers are really a defect here, as they make the operations slow and less effective. Smooth fingers are best.

MERCURY : The First phalanx longest indicates the possession of great power of expression, even eloquence and oratory. Public Speakers or Writers.
The Second phalanx longest make a good Doctor, Lawyer or Scientist.
The Third phalanx longest the commercial side will be the most prominent ; they are excellent merchants or business men in any capacity.
The First longest, with Pointed tip, the subject will be able to draw on his imagination, and will indulge in flights of fancy in oratory.
With Conic tip, will be artistic and eloquent, and will indulge in word painting and mental pictures.
With Square tip, they will talk on practical subjects, show commonsense and reason, while facts and figures will be employed freely.
With Spatulate tip, the subject will be a magnetic speaker, whose fiery oratory will move masses with its vigour or originality and strength.

The Second longest, with Pointed tip, idealism will permeate scientific researches.

Square tip, commonsense practical ideas rule.

Spatulate tip, active in search for fresh discoveries in old scenes ; will not be satisfied to follow beaten tracks.

THIRD LONGEST, WITH POINTED OR CONIC TIP, the idealism and love of the artistic will be linked to business ability.

Square tip, commonsense and practical ideas will operate and show a business man who makes every penny tell in his accounts, and brooks no foolishness in business matters.

Spatulate tip, great activity, energy and originality ; will push business and devise new way of making money. This is a strong combination.

In using these points on Individual Fingers, both hands must be compared, as in a very large number of hands the length and shape of the tips will vary. Thus in one hand the finger of Jupiter may be long and pointed, while in the other it may be shorter, with a Conic or Square tip thus indicating a very marked change in the individual —the long pointed Jupiter indicating a love of responsibility and with strong religious tendencies, whilst the shorter finger of Jupiter would tell of less liking for responsibility and a lessening of the religious tendencies, and in consequence a more practical condition of the mind.

The world teems with failures, many of whom could have successfully accomplished the work they were intended to do, but who, having been forced into avocations for which they were not designed, have grown discouraged at their non-success, have drifted on the lee-shores, and are now amongst the flotsam and jetsam of life-derelicts.

The pathway, purpose, successes and failures, are marked out for guidance and direction, and as a student of the greatest of all creative works—the human hand— I have, after many years of professional practice, no hesitaion in affirming that the Great Creator's chart is not only accurate, but readily discernable to the intelligent observer, and that obedience to its indications will ensure success.